Rotisserie Grilling

Mike Vrobel

CONTENTS

ACKNOWLEDGMENTS

Thank you, Diane. You are the love of my life.

Thank you, Ben, Natalie, and Tim, for putting up with dad making all these weird recipes.

Thank you to the rest of my family. I wouldn't be here without all the love and support you've given me.

Thank you for the proofreading prowess of Rhonda Estanich and Pam Semanik, and to the rest of our wine dinner group for all the great meals and years of friendship.

To everyone in the world of food who has influenced me - writers, chefs, bloggers, photographers, home cooks, farmers, ranchers, butchers, market goers, grillers and grill makers. This book is built on the shoulders of all those who went before me, and it wouldn't be here without your inspiration. Thank you all.

WHY ROTISSERIE?

I love gadgets. That's why I bought the rotisserie for my grill. It was a shiny new toy, and I had to have it. But the first time I used the rotisserie, I was asking myself "Why am I doing all this extra work?"

I had to:

1.   Truss the chicken with butcher's twine, so it wouldn't flop around, and then spear it with the rotisserie spit.

2.   Set up the rotisserie motor - dig the extension cord out of the garage, and run it across the deck to my grill.

3.   Wrestle a blazing hot stainless steel spear with a chicken stuck on it. When the spear came off the grill, it was a branding iron, waiting to sear any bare skin it could find.

I won't mention the tripped GFI outlet making me think the motor was dead. I also won't mention the poor trussing on the chicken, which needed an emergency loop of butcher's twine around the wings halfway through cooking. It was my first try, OK?

Why go through all that extra hassle? Because, after an hour on the rotisserie, I had a perfect roast chicken. It looked like the cover of a glossy food magazine, with crisp brown skin over the entire bird. The breast meat was juicy; the drumsticks and thighs were tender.

And then there were the wings. My wife loves chicken wings. She ate the first wing, then reached for another. Hesitating, she said: "These are so good...can I have both wings?" As I said "Sure", the wing was already on its way to her plate. The next time I made rotisserie chicken, my wife asked if I could cook an extra bird, just to get the extra set of wings. That's when I knew I had a winner.

Rotisserie grilling is worth the extra work; it just takes a little practice. Trussing and spitting a bird takes five minutes. The rotisserie motor and extension cord are easy to find, if I put them back where I found them. And I learned to be careful with the hot spit.

I bought a pair of welding gloves after I branded my wrist. Ouch.

There I was, a few months later, turning out perfect rotisserie chickens. I wondered what I could try next. I looked for new recipes, but they were few and far between. I thought a grilling cookbook was a success if it even mentioned the rotisserie. If the book had two or three recipes, I was ecstatic. I collected rotisserie recipes where I found them, but it wasn't enough. I started to experiment, trying different cuts of meat and translating roasting techniques to the rotisserie. You're looking at the result - the cookbook I was searching for all those years ago.

ROTISSERIE BASIC TECHNIQUE

Time to pull back the curtain and reveal the secrets behind this book. Rotisserie grilling isn't complicated; it is just another form of roasting. Once you learn the basic technique, the recipes get much easier. They become variations on a central theme. The heat level and timings are determined by what you're cooking. A thin loin roast that you want to cook medium-rare is cooked hot and fast. A thick shoulder roast needs time to become tender, and you want to cook it low and slow.

Here is the basic rotisserie technique:

1. Season the roast

2. Truss and spit the roast on the rotisserie spit

3. Pre-heat the grill, then set the grill up for indirect heat

4. Set the rotisserie spit in the rotisserie bracket, start the motor spinning, make sure the drip pan is centered under the food, and close the lid.

5. If cooking for more than an hour: On a charcoal grill, add coals every hour to keep the heat going. On a gas grill, turn the heat down a notch or two once the food is properly browned.

6. If there is a basting sauce or a glaze, brush it on during the last fifteen minutes of cooking.

7. Check if the food is done fifteen minutes before the suggested cooking time. When the food is cooked through, remove it from the spit, cut the trussing string loose, and let the roast rest for 15 minutes.

8. Carve and eat!

Cooking Temperature Chart

Type	Doneness	Temperature
Chicken (Measured in the breast)	Well Done	160°F
Chicken Legs	Well Done	180°F
Turkey (Measured in the breast)	Well Done	155°F
Cornish Hen (Measured in the breast)	Well Done	160°F
Duck (Measured in the breast)	Well Done	160°F
Pork Loin	Medium	135°F
Pork Shoulder	Well Done	190°F
Ham	Medium	135°F
Beef	Rare	115°F
Beef	Medium-Rare	120°F
Beef	Medium	130°F
Leg of Lamb	Medium	130°F
Lamb Shoulder	Medium	190°F

Timing Chart

Type	Thickness or Weight	Heat Level	Cooking Time
Chicken	4 pounds	Indirect High	1 hour
Cornish Hen	1.75 pounds	Indirect High	35 minutes
Turkey	12 pounds	Indirect Medium	2.5 hours
Turkey Breast	7 pounds	Indirect Medium	1.5 hours
Duck	5.5 pounds	Indirect High	1.5 hours
Pork Shoulder, boneless	4 pounds	Indirect Medium	1.5 hours
Pork Shoulder, bone-in	6 pounds	Indirect Medium	2.5 hours
Pork Loin, bone-in (Rack of Pork)	4 pounds	Indirect High	45 minutes
Pork Loin, boneless	2 (2 pound) roasts tied together	Indirect High	50 minutes
Pork Baby Back Ribs	1 slab	Indirect Medium	1.5 hours
Ham, Bone In	8 pounds	Indirect Medium-low	3 hours
Beef Prime Rib Roast	12 pounds (a 4 bone roast)	Indirect Medium-high	2 hours
Beef Prime Rib Roast	5 pounds (a 2 bone roast)	Indirect High	1 hour
Beef Ribeye Roast, boneless	4 pounds	Indirect High	1 hour
Beef Tenderloin	5 pound roast folded in half	Indirect High	50 minutes
Beef Sirloin Roast	4 pounds	Indirect High	45 minutes
Beef Back Ribs	1 slab	Indirect Medium	2 hours
Beef Tri-Tip Roast	2 pounds	Indirect High	20 minutes
Picanha (Top Sirloin cap roast)	3 pounds cut into 3 steaks	Indirect High	20 minutes
Leg of Lamb, whole, bone in	8 pounds	Indirect High	1.5 hours
Leg of Lamb roast, bone in	4 pounds	Indirect High	1 hour

Type	Thickness or Weight	Heat Level	Cooking Time
Leg of Lamb, boneless	2 1/2 pounds	Indirect High	45 minutes
Lamb Shoulder, boneless	4 pounds	Indirect Medium	2 hours
Lamb Chops	2 bone chops	Indirect High	15 minutes
Drip Pan Potatoes	1/2 inch slices	Indirect High	45 minutes
Drip Pan New Potatoes	Halved	Indirect High	45 minutes
Drip Pan Sweet Potatoes	Wedges	Indirect High	45 minutes
Onion	8 ounces	Indirect High	1 hour
Pineapple	1 Pound	Indirect High	1 hour

The Rotisserie Attachment

I'll start with the obvious: You need a rotisserie that fits your grill.

If the grill came with a rotisserie, you're all set. If not, check with the manufacturer. Most make a rotisserie attachment for their grills; if it is available, you want the rotisserie that was designed for your grill. If your manufacturer doesn't make a rotisserie, there are plenty of universal rotisseries that fit almost any grill.

Rotisseries are simple, with only a few parts:

* **Rotisserie spit:** a long metal spear, with notches to help it spin in the mounting bracket.

* **Spit forks:** A set of forks designed to slide onto the spit and lock down with thumbscrews. The forks secure the meat to the spit.

* **Mounting bracket:** There are two parts to the mounting bracket. One piece is the motor mount; a metal flange, about three inches across, that the motor sits on. The other piece is opposite the motor mount, and is simply a slot for the spit to rest on while it rotates. On my charcoal kettle, the mounting bracket is a large metal ring that fits between the grill's body and lid. There is a motor mount sticking out on one side, and a slot cut into the opposite side of the ring for the spit to rest on. For my gas grill the slots are built into the wall of the grill box, with the motor mount on the outside.

* **Rotisserie motor:** The motor fits on the mounting bracket, and has a socket the spit plugs into. When the motor is turned on, the socket rotates, spinning the rotisserie spit.

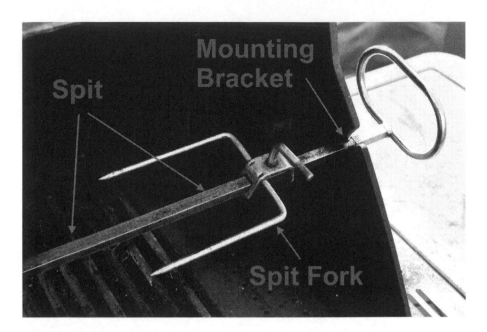

Spit

Mounting Bracket

Spit Fork

The Grill

For rotisserie grilling, the grill must be able to hold indirect high heat.

Indirect heat is necessary because a roast on a spit will drip fat into the same spot in the middle of the grill. If the fire is directly below the roast, it will soon be a roaring inferno of burning grease, and the roast will be covered with oily black soot.

High heat is needed to sear the outside of the food before it cooks through. When the grill is set up for indirect heat, it should 450°F. At lower temperatures the grill bakes the food without really browning, and the whole point of a rotisserie is that amazing browned crust.

The high heat rule applies to foods that cook for an hour or less. Larger roasts, like turkey, ribs, or shoulder cuts, brown at lower temperatures thanks to their long cooking time. If your grill is low on heat, and you really want to rotisserie, look at recipes that cook on medium heat for an hour and a half or longer.

Charcoal grills are easy to set up for indirect high heat. Burning charcoal generates a lot of heat. Pile the coals on the side of the grill and you are ready to go.

Cheap gas grills tend to be underpowered, and struggle to generate high heat. Good gas grills can hold 450°F with their middle burner turned off, so you can rotisserie over indirect heat. The best gas grills have a dedicated infrared rotisserie burner. These special burners, attached to the back wall of the grill box, focus heat right where the rotisserie needs it.

*You don't *need* a rotisserie burner for your gas grill, but it sure helps. My favorite gas grill is my huge Weber Summit. It has 6 regular burners plus a dedicated infrared rotisserie burner. It is expensive, and worth every penny I paid for it.*

Sidebar: Charcoal vs. Gas

The cheapest charcoal grill browns meat better than most gas grills. Why?

Warning! Science content ahead. If you want to skip it, the summary is: Meat browns as meat juices are exposed to heat and evaporate. Dry heat browns better than wet heat because the extra water has to evaporate before the meat will start to brown. Burning charcoal is dry heat. Burning gas releases water, making wet heat. Therefore, charcoal browns meat better than gas.

Starting science content. My wife, the high school chemistry teacher, made sure I have the science correct. She says you better not skip ahead. There will be a quiz.

Why is dry heat better than wet heat? The Maillard reaction.

The Maillard reaction occurs when sugars and amino acids are exposed to heat in a dry environment; the result is browning and the release of water. "The result is browning" is shorthand for complex chemical interactions that scientists are still figuring out. The sugars caramelize, interact with the amino acids, and produce all sorts of flavor compounds. Those flavor compounds are what make the browned crust on a roast so delicious.

Meat is full of protein fibers and meat juices. When meat is cooked, the heat tightens the muscle fibers, and they squeeze juices out of the meat. The meat juices are full of sugars and amino acids, and when they reach the surface of the meat, they are exposed to heat. That starts the Maillard reaction. As the juices brown, they release more water. That extra water slows down the Maillard reaction until it evaporates, and browning starts again.

Water prevents browning. Meat needs to be cooked at 350°F or higher to evaporate the water fast enough to keep the browning reaction going, and higher temperatures are better. Boiled meat is gray, without any browning at all, because it is covered with water. This is why recipes recommend patting food dry before cooking; any extra water slows down browning until it evaporates.

Now we get to charcoal versus gas. (Finally!)

Charcoal is wood heated in an oxygen free environment. When all the water in the wood has evaporated, you are left with carbon. When carbon is burned, it produces heat, carbon dioxide, and a little carbon monoxide. That's our dry heat - no water.

Gas is either propane or methane (also known as natural gas). When gas is burned, it produces heat, carbon dioxide, and water. That water is the problem - it needs to be evaporated by the heat of the grill before the Maillard reaction will start.

Now for the good news: a rotisserie helps browning, whether you use gas or charcoal. Escaping juices roll around the surface of the meat, spreading the sugars and amino acids so the Maillard reaction can do its thing. Yes, a charcoal grill with a rotisserie browns better than a gas grill with a rotisserie. But, a gas grill with a rotisserie browns about as well as a charcoal grill without a rotisserie. If you have a gas grill, don't give up - the rotisserie will still help.

End Science content. You can keep reading now.

If you want a gas grill that browns as well as a charcoal grill, you need more heat, to help evaporate the extra water. This means more burners, especially infrared burners, which do a great job of generating heat. But that makes the grill more expensive. It's tough to beat a cheap kettle grill filled with charcoal.

Don't get me wrong; I use both charcoal and gas grills. In a perfect world, I would use charcoal all the time. However...gas grills are so convenient. They're easy to light and provide constant, even heat as long as you don't run out of gas. There are no worries about charcoal burning down and cooling off; there's no need to add extra coals every hour. In the middle of February, when every trip to the grill involves shoveling snow, I love that extra convenience.

Setting up a grill for rotisserie grilling.

Here are the temperatures I shoot for when I'm rotisserie grilling:

Heat	Temperature
High	450°F or higher
Medium-High	400°F
Medium	350°F
Medium-Low	300°F
Low	250°F

You need to experiment with your grill to find the burner settings (or amount of charcoal) that give you these temperatures. As I said earlier, if your grill can't hold a temperature of 350°F when set up for indirect heat, it's probably not good for rotisserie grilling. 450°F is ideal, and more power is always better.

Charcoal grill setup

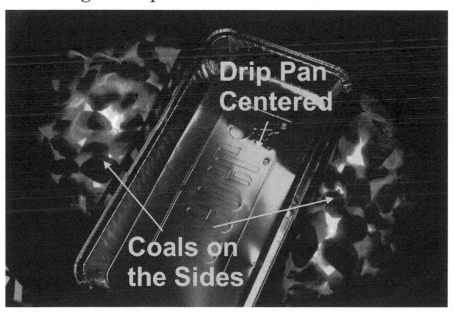

Drip Pan Centered

Coals on the Sides

1. Remove the grill grate and set it aside.

The drip pan and the rotating meat need space, and most grills don't have enough clearance without removing the grate.

2. Light the charcoal.

The amount of charcoal controls the heat. I light 5 quarts of charcoal (about 60 briquettes) for high heat on a 22-inch kettle grill. This is the exact amount a Weber charcoal chimney holds if filled to the top. For medium heat, light 4 1/2 quarts of charcoal/45 briquettes/75 percent of the Weber charcoal chimney; for low heat, use 3 quarts of charcoal/30 briquettes/half of the charcoal chimney. Charcoal is ready when the coals are mostly covered by gray ash, with just a little of the black coal still showing.

I start my grill with a charcoal chimney. Fill the chimney with charcoal, stuff two crumpled pieces of newspaper in the bottom, light the paper, and the coals are ready in about 20 minutes. In windy conditions, I spray a little vegetable oil on the paper to make sure it stays lit. Other good ways to start charcoal are electric starters and wax fire starter cubes. Stay away from lighter fluid. Supposedly it burns off, leaving you with nothing but the flavor of the charcoal, but I can smell it whenever it's been used. I don't want that flavor in my food. And never, EVER use instant light charcoal. It is soaked through with lighter fluid. No matter how long it burns, it will always give off that butane smell.

3. Set up the grill.

Pour the coals in two even piles on the sides of the grill. If your grill has charcoal baskets, use them. Charcoal burns better in a tight pile than if the coals are spread out, and a basket holds the coals together. Set the drip pan in the middle, between the piles of charcoal.

4. Assemble the rotisserie.

Slide the rotisserie motor onto the motor mount. Plug the end of the spit into the motor, and set the spit into the rotisserie bracket. Start the motor and make sure the spit is spinning freely. Center the drip pan beneath the roast and shut the lid. Keep the lid closed as much as possible - no peeking!

5. Re-fuel the grill.

Charcoal burns out in about an hour and a half. If the roast will cook for longer than an hour, add more coals every hour to keep the fire going. For high heat, add 24 briquettes every hour. For medium add 16 briquettes; for low, add 12 briquettes. Split the extra coals evenly between the charcoal piles on the sides of the grill.

Gas grill setup

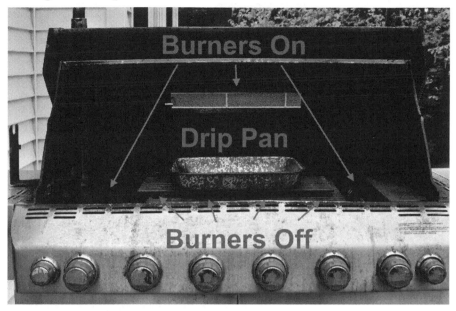

Burners On

Drip Pan

Burners Off

1. Remove the grill grates.

The drip pan and the rotating meat need space. Most grills don't have enough clearance without removing the grates.

Turkey and other large roasts may need even more space. If the big bird is brushing up against the burner covers, remove them and set the drip pan directly on the (unlit) burner. Remember to put the burner covers back when you're done; your grill needs them for regular grilling.

2. Preheat the grill for 15 minutes with all burners on high.

The grill should be hot before any food goes inside.

3. Turn off the burners in the middle of the grill, and turn on the rotisserie burner if you have one.

This is where different grill setups come into play. On three burner grills, the two outside burners are lit and the inside burner is off. Four burner grills have two outside burners lit, two inside burners off. Six burner grills have two outside burners lit, four inside burners off.

(Those are the usual burner configurations; if you have something different, just follow the pattern.)

If your grill has an infrared rotisserie burner, turn it on now. Infrared burners heat up very quickly, so they don't need pre-heating time.

Once the grill is set up for indirect heat, adjust the burners that are still lit to get the heat level you need for the recipe.

4. Put the drip pan over the unlit burners.

5. Assemble the rotisserie

Slide the rotisserie motor onto the motor mount. Plug the end of the spit into the motor, and set the spit into the rotisserie bracket. Start the motor and make sure the spit is spinning freely. Center the drip pan beneath the roast and shut the lid. Keep the lid closed unless it is absolutely necessary - Rotisserie grilling works best when the lid is closed, especially on a gas grill.

Charcoal burn down, and simulating it on a gas grill

When cooking on a gas grill, the temperature stays where you set it. High heat means 450°F, and it stays there for as long as you cook. Charcoal does not have a constant heat level. It starts at 450°F and drops as the charcoal burns down. This is a good thing; you start with high heat for good browning, then the heat ramps down. The roast cooks through without burning on the outside, and finishing with lower heat leaves more juices inside the meat.

You can simulate this burn-down effect with a gas grill. If you have an infrared rotisserie burner this may be mandatory; constant high heat from the rotisserie burner can burn the food before it cooks through. On a gas grill, check the roast after a half hour of cooking. If it is browned enough, or starting to blacken in spots, turn down the heat.

Smoking wood

Wood smoke adds another layer of flavor when cooking on the rotisserie. There are a variety of smoking woods, and the flavor differences between most of them are subtle. Hickory is the most common, but other good smoking woods are oak, apple, cherry, pecan, alder and maple. Stay away from pine and mesquite; pine burns with a resinous smoke and mesquite has a bitter flavor.

*My current favorite is oak wine barrel staves cut from decommissioned wine barrels. Their fermenting grape smell takes me back to wine country.

Smoking wood can be purchased in chunks or chips; use chunks with charcoal grills, and chips with gas grills.

Soak smoking wood in water for an hour before cooking. Damp wood smolders and releases more smoke than dry wood. Drain the wood right before using it and put it in the grill when you start cooking the roast. The soaking step is critical for chips, because un-soaked wood chips will go up in a flash. For wood chunks, soaking is optional.

Adding wood to a charcoal grill is easy - just put a fist-sized piece of wood directly on the coals. The chunks I get at my local hardware store are a range of sizes, and the big pieces are the perfect size. But, when I get to the bottom of the bag, I need to use two or three smaller pieces to match the size of my fist.

For gas grills use one cup of soaked wood chips. If there is a dedicated smoker on the grill, put the chips in the smoker box and turn on the smoker burner. If you don't have a smoker box, make an aluminum foil envelope of wood chips. Lay the chips in a single layer on a piece of heavy-duty aluminum foil and fold the foil around them to make a flat package. Poke a few holes in the foil so smoke can escape. Set the envelope of wood chips under the grill grate, on the burner cover directly above a lit burner.

In general, gas grills don't smoke as well as charcoal grills. (Yes, here's another charcoal grill advantage.) Burning propane or methane releases a lot of combustion gases, so gas grills are built with air vents to let those gases escape. Unfortunately, those vents let the wood smoke escape with the combustion gases. The smoke leaves the grill before it gets much of a chance to flavor the food. That said, don't skip the wood when gas grilling; a little smoke flavor is better than nothing.

SEASONING BASICS

Salt

Salting food properly is the key to cooking. A rotisserie chicken, seasoned with nothing but salt, is one of my favorite meals.

Salt brings out the flavor of food and smooths out bitter tastes. Too little salt, and food tastes bland; the right amount of salt makes food taste like itself - only more so. Of course, it can be overdone - too much salt and the food is inedible. Luckily, there's a wide window between enough salt and too much salt.

Most people are less sensitive to salt than they think they are. You'd be amazed how much salt is sprinkled on food in restaurants, and even more amazed at how much salt is in canned and processed food. That said, if your doctor told you to cut back on salt...cut back on salt. Focus on the recipes with spice rubs and spice pastes instead.

I season by hand, sprinkling roasts with big pinches of salt. I use kosher salt, because it has large, flaky grains that make it easy to pinch. Grabbing a big pinch of table salt is impossible - the tiny grains escape, leaving me with a few grains of salt squeezed between my thumb and fingertips.

Also, the large flakes of kosher salt weigh less than the same amount of table salt, making it harder to over-salt food.

Now, what do I mean, kosher salt weights less than table salt? It's all about the density of different salt crystals. Table salt has small, dense crystals;

kosher salt has large, airy flakes. Because we measure salt by volume (teaspoons, tablespoons, cups) instead of weight, density is important. A tablespoon of table salt weighs twice as much as a tablespoon of kosher salt.

Salt Type	Weight of 1 cup (ounces)	Percent of Diamond Crystal kosher
Table Salt	11	50%
Pickling Salt	11	50%
Coarse Sea Salt	9	75%
Fine Sea Salt	9	75%
Morton's kosher Salt	9	75%
Diamond Crystal kosher Salt	6	100%

All my recipes use Diamond Crystal brand kosher salt. It is inexpensive, widely available, and has light, flaky crystals that are easy to work with. If you can't find Diamond Crystal kosher, use the percentage column to convert the recipe to the salt you have. In general, cut the salt in half when using table salt or pickling salt. If you use sea salt or Morton's kosher salt, use 3/4 of the amount in the recipe.

Seasoning Styles

Salt and Pepper

It's simple and traditional. Sprinkle your roast with salt and pepper right before cooking.

Seasoning before cooking is more effective than seasoning after cooking. As the food cooks, the salt dissolves in the cooking juices, becoming part of the crisp, brown crust.

After rambling on about the weight of salt, I'm afraid to start with pepper...but I can't help myself. Black pepper tastes best fresh ground. A lot of the pepper flavor is in volatile oils, which start to escape when the peppercorn is cracked. Pre-ground pepper is a shadow of fresh ground, so invest in a good pepper mill and grind pepper right when you need it.

Brines, both Wet and Dry

Brining is one of the big advances in home cooking over the last decade.

Brining seasons a roast all the way through, not just on the surface. When meat is soaked in salt water, two things happen:

  9.   Salt and water are pulled deep into the meat through osmosis.

10. Salt denatures protein, changing its structure. Denatured protein bonds well with water molecules, so the meat holds more water than it did before.

The deep penetration of salt is a good thing, but the extra water retained by the meat is a mixed blessing. Lean meat can use that extra water, especially when cooked to higher temperatures. Lean meat doesn't have fat to keep it juicy, so the extra water helps prevent the meat from drying out. But, the extra water also dilutes the flavor of the meat and slows down browning. (Remember our discussion on browning and dry environments? Sure you do.)

Dry brining has the deep seasoning of wet brining, without adding water. When a roast is salted, osmosis pulls juices out of the meat. Those salty juices sit on the surface, and if you wait long enough, a brining effect starts to happen, and the salt and meat juices are pulled back into the meat. The meat is brining in its own juices! As a bonus, some of the water evaporates from the juices before they are pulled back in, concentrating the flavor of the meat.

When to dry brine, when to wet brine

Dry brines are easier, but take longer. You can get a bit of a dry brine effect in an hour, but it works better if the roast is salted at least eight hours before you want to cook it. Let the roast sit in the refrigerator overnight, or for up to three days, for the best dry brine experience.

Wet brines are messier and quicker. You need enough brine to completely submerge the meat. That much water is heavy, hard to move without sloshing around, and takes up a lot of room in the refrigerator. On the plus side, wet brines are quicker than dry brines. A concentrated wet brine can season a roast in one to four hours.

So, which brining method should you use? I did taste tests with different meats, comparing dry brines, wet brines, and salting the meat right before cooking, to come up with an answer.

Beef and lamb taste better with a dry brine. If I don't have time for a dry brine, I prefer to salt them right before cooking. Beef and lamb taste waterlogged with a wet brine.

Poultry tastes better with a dry brine, so I try to make the time for one. I will use a wet brine on poultry if I'm in a hurry; poultry tastes better with a wet brine than with no brine at all.

Pork tastes better wet brined. I think pork needs the extra water retained by a wet brine. If I don't have time to wet brine, then I definitely don't have time to dry brine, so I salt the pork right before cooking.

My recipes reflect these preferences - most of my pork recipes are wet brined, and almost all the other recipes are dry brined. If you're in a hurry, don't worry about brining - season the meat right before putting it on the grill.

There is one other problem with dry brining. A brine is a salt water solution - no water, no brine. Dry brining is really early salting, or salt curing. The phrase "dry brine" explains how it works...but is not technically correct. Forgive me for using the simple explanation, even if it is wrong.

Marinades and Brinerades

Marinades are another traditional seasoning method - soaking meat in a flavorful liquid. The problem is, unlike brines, marinades are not absorbed into the meat. Marinades season a very thin layer on the outside of the meat, regardless of how long you marinate.

There arc a couple of exceptions. The first is high acid marinades. If the marinade has a lot of vinegar or citrus juice, it will cook the outside of the meat. (Think of a Mexican ceviche where seafood is cooked by soaking it in lime juice.) We don't want acid to cook our meat; if it happens, it means the meat was marinated for too long.

The second exception is pineapple. Pineapple contains an enzyme, bromelain, which breaks down proteins. Bromclain is the primary ingredient in commercial meat tenderizers. Marinating with pineapple will definitely tenderize meat, but lcave it soaking too long and the meat turns mushy.

In general, I don't marinate, I brinerate. (Yes, there I go again, messing with the definition of brining.) If a marinade has a high proportion of salt, it will work like a brine and the salt will work its way into the meat. Unfortunately, the flavors in the marinade don't penetrate with the salt. They stay on the surface of the meat. That's OK; the layer of flavor on the outside combined with a deep seasoning of salt is a great combination.

Spice rubs and spice pastes

Spice rubs and spice pastes are another way to season food. Their goal is quick coating of spice on the outside of the meat, without a lot of effort.

Spice rubs are dry, and the spices are usually mixed with herbs, salt, and sometimes sugar. Spice rubs are sprinkled and "rubbed" onto the meat to help them stick. But, If I rub too much, all the spices wind up on my fingers instead of the meat. Instead of rubbing, I sprinkle the meat with rub, and then pat and press it gently to help it stick.

Spice pastes are wet. They are made with a base of vegetable oil, mixed with fresh herbs, garlic, and dried spices. The result is a thick paste to spread over the roast.

Bastes and sauces

Bastes and sauces are liquids that are brushed on towards the end of cooking, to add another layer of flavor to the roast.

Bastes have a lot of fat in them; the simplest baste is the drippings from the roast itself. Rotisserie cooking is self-basting; when juices start to drip from the meat, they roll around the outside for a while before falling into the drip pan.

We can help a rotisserie's built in basting with melted butter. Butter contains milk proteins, which act like the meat's own juices and help the browning process. I add herbs and spices to my butter bastes; If I'm going to melt the butter, why not add some extra flavors?

Sauces are liquids that combine salt, acid, or sugar. A simple sauce is a squeeze of lemon juice at the last minute, adding a burst of bright acid. Barbecue sauce is a more complex example, combining tomatoes, spices, vinegar and sugar.

A lot of sauces have sugar in them, so they will add a thick, sweet glaze to a roast. You have to watch out, though, because sugar will burn in the high heat of a grill. I wait until the last fifteen minutes of cooking to add sugary sauces. That's just enough time for the sugar to caramelize, turning the sauce into a glaze, but not enough time for the sugar to burn.

TRUSSING AND SPITTING

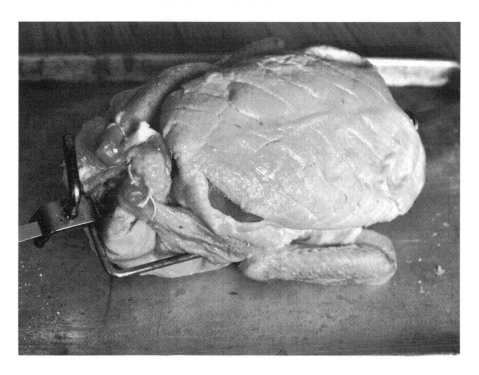

Why truss a roast?

Food spinning on the rotisserie wants to wobble around and break loose from the spit. Trussing holds the food in a tight, even shape.

Trussing is done with butcher's twine, a heavy, food safe string made out of cotton or linen. I've heard that linen is better for roasting, because it does not brown or burn when heated. But linen twine is expensive, and I'm too cheap. I buy cotton twine and live with a little browning on the edges.

Note - do not use colorful "baking twine", or any twine with nylon in it for cooking. Nylon melts, and you don't want melted plastic on your food.

The surgeon's knot

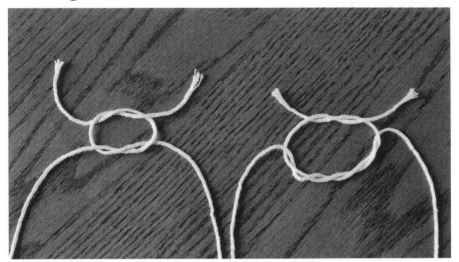

Square knot on the left, Surgeon's knot on the right.

A surgeon's knot is useful to know when trussing. It is a square knot with two extra loops added to the first tie.

A square knot is tied like this: make the first tie by crossing the ends of the twine, then loop one end over the other and pull tight. Make a second tie by crossing and looping the ends again, then pull tight to finish the knot.

For a surgeon's knot, start like a square knot, and cross the ends of the twine and loop one end over the other. Then, loop the end over two more times before pulling tight. Those extra two loops add tension to the first tie, holding it tight while you finish the knot with the second tie. The extra tension also holds the food in the shape you want. As an example, a roast is pulled into a round shape when you tighten the first tie, and the extra loops in the surgeon's knot hold that shape while you finish tying the knot.

Trussing and spitting poultry

Trussing poultry is tricky. Poultry has wings, legs, and drumsticks sticking out everywhere, and they need to be tied into a tight package for the rotisserie. This trussing technique works on all types of poultry, from the smallest Cornish hen up to the largest turkey.

Trussing poultry

Cut a piece of twine four times the length of the bird. Fold the wingtips tight under the bird; this locks them in place, so they won't flop around on the grill. Set the bird on its backbone, with the drumsticks pointing at you and the breast and wings away from you. Find the middle of the piece of twine, reach around to the front of the bird, and loop that middle over the nub of the neck. Wrap both sides of the twine around the breast, just above the wing, and bring them together at the cavity behind the bird. Tie a surgeon's knot at the cavity, pulling the knot tight to plump up the breast. Next, tie the drumsticks. Take the ends of the twine in both hands and bring them down between the knobs of the drumsticks. Loop them out and up to catch the knobs, then pull the knobs of the drumsticks together by tying the first part of a surgeon's knot. Keep tightening the knot and pushing on the knobs until they cross, forming an X. Continue to tighten the knot and push the knobs towards the cavity until the drumsticks are up against the first knot. Tie off the surgeon's knot and trim any extra twine.

Spitting poultry

Tighten the first spit fork on the spit. Run the spit through the bird, starting at the cavity in the back, and sink the forks into the thighs. Slide the second spit fork on to the spit and push the fork into the bird's breast meat just above the wings. Keep pushing until the bird is squeezed between both forks. Make sure the bird is centered on the spit, then tighten the second fork to lock the bird in place. That's it - the bird is ready for the rotisserie.

Trussing Poultry Step By Step

Tuck the wings under the bird.

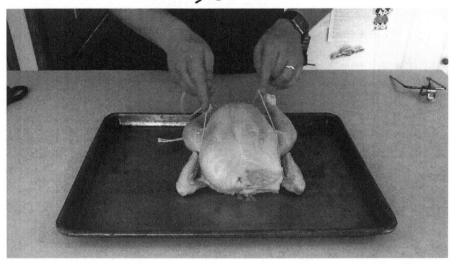

Loop the middle of the twine over the nub of the neck, wrap around the sides of the breast, and tie a knot behind the cavity, pulling tight to plump up the breast.

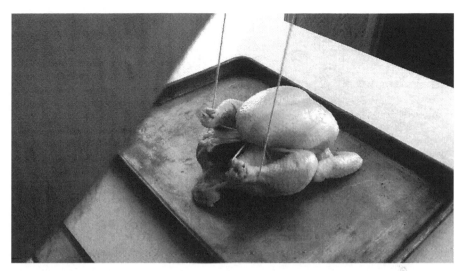

Loop the ends of the twine under the knobs of the drumsticks, then...

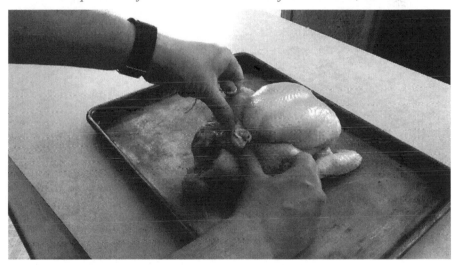

...tie another knot, pushing the knobs to cross, and pull tight against the first knot.

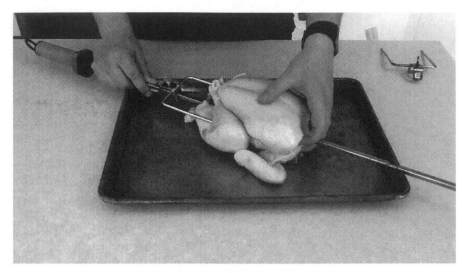

Run the spit through the bird, pushing one fork deep into the thighs, and the other just above the wings.

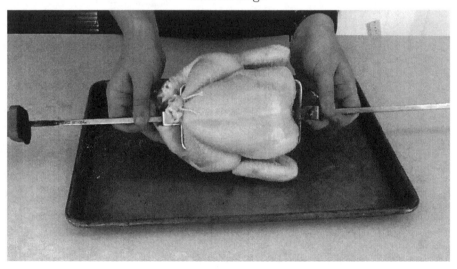

Ready for the grill.

Trussing and spitting roasts

Roasts want to be a wobbly oval on the spinning rotisserie. Trussing them into a tight cylinder helps roasts cook evenly. Roasts are easier to truss than poultry. A roast is trussed every inch and a half to two inches along its length to hold it in shape as the spit turns.

Trussing roasts

If the roast is a large muscle of meat, like a loin, it only needs to be trussed to hold it in a tight cylinder. A truss pulled tight every two inches along the length will be fine.

Roasts with less structure need more trussing. Deboned leg roasts are a great example - with their central bone removed, they don't have any structure. These roasts should be folded or rolled into their original shape, then trussed every inch and a half to hold them together on the spit.

The bones in bone-in roasts hold them together, so they don't need to be tied as tightly. One truss between every bone is enough, even if it is two to three inches between bones.

Spitting roasts

To spit a roast, lock the first spit fork on the spit, then run the spit through the center of the roast. If the roast is thick enough, push the tines of the fork into the roast to hold it steady; if the roast is narrower, use the fork as cage around the meat. Slide the second fork onto the spit and secure the other end of the roast. Make sure the roast is centered, then lock down the second fork. You're done - the roast is ready for the grill.

Trussing Roasts Step By Step

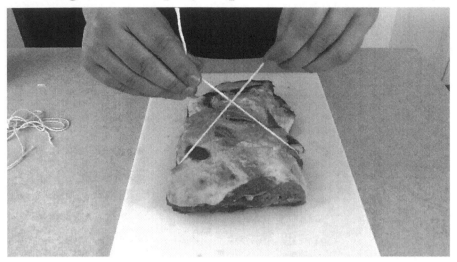

Tying the first surgeon's knot.

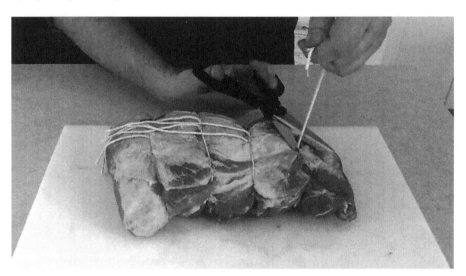

Trussed every 2 inches.

Run the spit through the center of the roast.

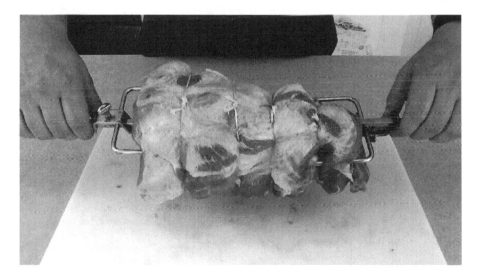

Ready for the grill.

COOKING ON THE ROTISSERIE

The grill is lit, with smoking wood added to the coals. The roast is seasoned, trussed, and spinning over the drip pan. Congratulations! You're rotisserie grilling. Enjoy a tasty beverage and keep that lid closed.

Check the grill after 30 minutes to make sure everything is still spinning and up to temperature. Other than that, keep the lid closed until it is time to check for doneness.

Unless you are cooking on a charcoal grill for over an hour. Then you need to add more coals every hour on the hour.

Fifteen minutes before the suggested cooking time, check the temperature of the roast. Insert an instant read thermometer in the thickest part of the meat, staying away from the rotisserie spit. (The spit will be hotter than the roast, and it can throw the reading off.) The roast should not be done yet - if it isn't, close the lid and continue to cook. At this point, how often you check the food depends on how close it was to done. If the food was really close, check it again in five minutes; if not, check it again in fifteen minutes, at the suggested cooking time. When the roast reaches the proper internal temperature, it's done.

About cooking times

An instant read thermometer is the best way to answer: "Is it done yet?"

I cook tender cuts of beef to medium-rare, and tender cuts of pork and lamb to medium. Medium-rare is a warm, red center with an internal temperature of 125°F; medium is a warm, pink center with an internal temperature of 140°F. The tricky part is carry-over cooking. When the roast is removed from the grill, the outside of the meat is hotter than the inside. That heat continues to cook the inside of the roast. To adjust my temperature for that extra cooking time, I give myself an extra five degrees. So, for medium-rare, the roast comes off the grill at 120°F. After a fifteen minute rest it will be a perfect 125°F. For medium, I pull the roast at 135°F.

For safety, cook poultry to 160°F, measured in the thickest part of the breast. That temperature kills salmonella instantly. The problem is white meat. The meat in poultry breasts is so lean that it is already drying out at 160°F. You want to get the bird off the grill the moment it reaches 160. The longer you wait, the drier the breast meat. Poultry legs have more fat and connective tissue; cook them between 170°F to 180°F to make them tender. Luckily, trussing forces the legs to stick out and cook quicker than the breast. The legs will be the right temperature when the breast reaches 160°F.

Then there are tougher cuts, usually from the shoulder. The tough connective tissue starts to melt at 160°F and become tender gelatin. It's almost impossible to overcook shoulder cuts; the longer they cook, the better they are. I cook them to 190°F for the most tender results.

The Big Lie in every cookbook is cooking times. (Yes, even this one.) All cooking times are, at best, approximations. Let's take rotisserie chicken as an example. A four pound chicken will be cooked to 160°F in the thickest part of the breast after one hour on the rotisserie over high heat...under ideal conditions.

Conditions are rarely ideal. What if the chicken is 3 1/2 pounds, not four pounds? Maybe this bird has a particularly thick breast. It could be a windy day, pulling heat out of the grill. Perhaps I was in a hurry and kept opening the lid to check the food. All this adds up to changes in the time to cook.

That's just in my own back yard. Your grill is almost certainly different from mine, even if it's a typical kettle grill. We're cooking with live fire, and every fire turns out different. (If you cook with charcoal, you're nodding your head right now.) If you have a gas grill, remember that you're cooking in the great outdoors, and weather can have an effect.

All my recipes list a temperature that I consider "done." Then I'll suggest a cooking time. Trust the temperature, but not the time. My "about an hour" for a rotisserie chicken may be fifty minutes for you, or it may be an hour and five minutes.

I always check my food a half an hour into the cook, and fifteen minutes before it is supposed to be done. I get an idea of how quickly the roast is cooking...and I can adjust the expectations for dinnertime.

The amazing thing is, even with all those variations, I can put a four pound chicken over high heat, start the rotisserie spinning, and an hour later the chicken will probably be ready to serve.

After the food is done

When the food is done cooking, immediately remove the spit from the grill, the food from the spit, and the trussing twine from the food. The heat radiating from the spit will continue to cook the roast, even when it's not on the grill - get it off the spit quickly, or it will overcook.

The trussing twine also needs to come off right away, because it is easier to remove twine from a hot roast. Once the outside of the roast cools down, the crust will solidify, sticking to the twine. At that point, removing the twine will also rip off big chunks of the crust.

Please use oven mitts or grilling gloves while you work with the hot spit! The spit and forks are branding irons when they come off the grill. Loosen the spit forks with pliers or tongs, then slide the roast off the spit onto a large platter and remove the forks from the meat.

Finally, let the roast sit at room temperature for ten to fifteen minutes before carving. The meat's muscle fibers tighten up in the heat of the grill. If the roast is cut right away, the tight muscle fibers will squeeze juices out, and the roast won't be moist. If you let the roast cool before carving, the muscle fibers relax, and those juices will stay in the meat.

Bonus science content - muscle fibers start to tighten up at 120°F. For the juiciest results, let the roast rest until it cools down below 120°F. Now, I pay a lot of attention to the cooking temperature, but not much to the cooling temperature. I know...shame on me. It usually takes me fifteen minutes to get the side dishes together. I carve the roast as the last step, right before calling everyone to the table, and take it on faith that it is cooled below 120°F.

USEFUL EQUIPMENT

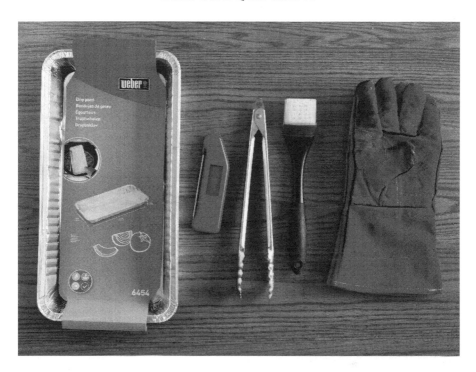

The essentials

We've already talked about the basics: a grill with a rotisserie attachment and trussing twine. Here are the other things you need.

Drip pans

Fat and juices drip constantly from a roast cooking on a rotisserie. Drip pans keep the bottom of the grill clean and prevent grease fires.

Disposable aluminum foil pans are the easiest solution. They are available in a wide range of sizes, and cleanup is simple - just throw away the grease filled pan. Buying foil pans one at a time at the grocery store is expensive, at a dollar or more per pan. Check your local warehouse store or restaurant supply store, because buying in bulk can bring the per-pan cost down dramatically. Look for packs of 9-inch by 13-inch "half-size steam table pans" which are perfect for use in the grill.

Using an aluminum foil pan once and throwing it away seems wasteful, but grills are rough on cookware. High heat scorches and warps pans, soot stains them, and juices burn in the drip pan, leaving a real mess.

I do use foil pans more than once, if they're not too messy, and I'm not cooking a drip pan side dish.

I found another option - enameled steel pans. Enameled steel is tough enough to handle the heat of the grill, easy to clean, and inexpensive. Inexpensive is important. Eventually, the heat of the grill destroys the pan, and I don't feel bad about replacing it.

The red speckled pan you see in most of my pictures is a 9-inch by 13-inch enameled steel baking pan. It has lasted three grilling seasons so far, and looks like it will be good for at least a few more before I have to replace it.

If you are desperate for a drip pan, you can improvise with aluminum foil. Tear off a big piece, fold it over, then crimp the edges into a pan shape and you are ready to roll. When you're done cooking, let the grill cool off completely before removing a homemade foil pan. Once the fat solidifies you can fold it up and toss it.

Don't use a homemade pan with something that generates a lot of fat, like a duck. It's a real mess if the pan collapses due to the weight of the fat.

Heat proof gloves

Handling a hot metal spit straight off the grill is a great way to burn yourself. Protect your hands, please. You can get by with oven mitts, but heatproof gloves are a better choice. Buy a pair of gloves designed for grilling, or do what I do and get a pair of welding gloves from the hardware store.

Don't forget that the spit fork knobs are as hot as the spit itself. Burnt fingertips aren't fun.

Instant read thermometer

Internal temperature is the best way to tell if food is cooked properly. Instant read thermometers have a thin metal probe, and read temperatures...well, not instantly, but quickly. The best instant read thermometers are digital models with a thermocouple in the tip; they are expensive, accurate, and fast - they read temperatures in four seconds. (Look for the Thermapen by Thermoworks. It costs about $100, and is worth it.) Less expensive digital thermometers work in about 30 seconds, and aren't as accurate. Analog thermometers are cheap, slow, and usually have small, hard to read dials.

Get the best thermometer that fits your budget. A $7.00 analog thermometer from the grocery store is far better than the alternatives - guessing doneness by wiggling thighs, cutting and peeking with a paring knife, or waiting for the juices to run clear.

Things that aren't absolutely necessary, but make rotisserie grilling easier

Spring-loaded kitchen tongs

Tongs are my hands while I cook. Tongs let me grab hot things that I don't want to touch with my grungy heat-proof gloves. I use them to re-arrange drip pan potatoes, pull spit forks out of roasts, and push chickens off the spit.

Basting brushes

I do a lot of basting, and I always use silicone basting brushes. A silicone brush covered with barbecue sauce goes straight into the dishwasher and comes out looking brand new.

Carving board and serving platter

Most rotisserie cooking involves a large roast, which needs to be carved and served. A carving board has more surface area than a typical cutting board, and most carving boards come with a deep juice well around the outside.

A large serving platter is the natural companion to a carving board. Move the carved roast to the platter, dump the juices from the carving board over the roast, and it's time to serve.

Carving knives

I do most of my carving and slicing with my eight inch chef's knife, the workhorse of my kitchen. I have a long slicing knife and an electric carving knife, both of which are rarely used. A long, sharp knife that you feel comfortable using is the only requirement for carving.

Kitchen scissors

There is a lot of trussing twine to cut while rotisserie cooking, so a pair of heavy-duty kitchen scissors is almost a requirement. A good pair will also work as poultry shears when it is time to break down a rotisserie chicken. Get a pair that can be separated into two halves; they are easy to clean after working with raw meat.

ROTISSERIE FAQ

Q: What's the first thing I should cook on my rotisserie?

A: Start with a <u>Chicken with Basic Dry Brine</u> - cook two chickens if you're feeding a crowd. Next, try <u>Pork Shoulder with Basic Wet Brine</u> or <u>Cornish Hens with Tex-Mex Rub, Stuffed with Lime and Herbs</u>. Then try <u>Prime Rib Roast</u> or <u>Turkey with Basic Dry Brine</u>, especially if you're near a major holiday. After that it's up to you - look through the recipes and pick one that calls out to you.

Q: I only have two spit forks. Can I cook two chickens?

A: Absolutely. Use the forks to push the chickens tightly together before locking them down. But make sure they're tight - otherwise, the chickens will work loose while they are spinning on the grill. Trying to re-skewer loose chickens with hot spit forks over a pile of lit coals is not fun.

Q: My grill has an infrared rotisserie burner. When should I use it?

A: You should use it every time you use the rotisserie...almost.

When the recipe calls for indirect high heat, you want the infrared rotisserie burner on, because the internal temperature of the grill should be 450°F or higher.

For indirect medium or lower temperatures, it depends on how hot your grill gets with the infrared burner. Using indirect medium as an example: you want a 350°F internal temperature, and should adjust your infrared burner and grill burners to hold that temperature. On my Weber Summit I get that temperature by setting burners 1 and 6 to medium and the IR rotisserie burner to medium.

Q: I want to use smoking wood with a recipe, but you don't mention it. Should I?

A: Absolutely! Smoke is a welcome addition to any recipe in this book. I only mention it in recipes where smoke is essential to the flavor, but don't let that stop you from adding it to other recipes.

Q: I forgot to dry brine the day before. Is it too late?

A: Two hours is long enough to get a dry brine effect. If you're within an hour or two of cooking, skip the dry brine. That is the window of time where salt pulls juices out of the meat, but osmosis doesn't have time to re-absorb them, resulting in drier meat.

For beef and lamb, I will dry brine up to two hours before cooking. For poultry, if I forget to dry brine the night before, I use a wet brine. If I'm really absent-minded that day, and miss the two hour window, I season the roast right before it goes on the rotisserie. I don't get the deep seasoning of a brine, but the roast will still taste great.

Q: Why do you take meat out of the refrigerator so early?

A: A roast straight from the refrigerator won't cook as evenly as one at room temperature. The inside of a refrigerated roast is starting at 40°F; the outside of the meat will overcook by the time the center is properly cooked.

Is it the end of the world if you don't take the roast out of the refrigerator early? No, of course not. The results will still be good. But the roast will cook more evenly if it is at room temperature when you start.

Q: I don't have a rotisserie for my grill. Can I make any of the recipes in this book?

A: Wow, I'm flattered you read this far. You really should get a rotisserie; the results are worth it. But, if a rotisserie is out of reach for now, you can still make all the recipes in this book. Set the grill up for indirect heat with a drip pan as described in the recipe. Put the grill grate back on the grill and set the meat on the grate over the drip pan. Start poultry breast side down; flip breast side up halfway through the cooking time. Start roasts fat side up, and leave them that way until they are done. Other than that, the recipes work as written - they take about the same amount of time, maybe a little longer. Use an instant read thermometer to check if the roast is done.

Q: I don't have a grill. Can I make any of the recipes in this book?

A: Mom, is that you? You must be a relative if you're reading a book about rotisserie grilling and don't own a rotisserie.

Oh, well, we'll give it a try. All the recipes can be cooked in an oven; put the roast in a rack over a roasting pan, and cook at the suggested temperatures (450°F for high, 350°F for medium). Start poultry breast side down, and flip halfway through; cook other roasts with the fatty side facing up. Cooking will take a little longer without the convection effect of the rotisserie, so use an instant read thermometer to figure out when the roast is done.

Q: What about countertop electric rotisseries? I saw a great deal on late night television...

A: I'm sorry, but I've never tried one. If the countertop rotisserie can hold the oven temperatures from the previous answer, it should work. Good luck, and drop me a line if you try it, to let me know how it goes.

Q: What do you have against gas grills, you charcoal snob?

A: I admit, I'm a reformed charcoal snob. I do prefer cooking with charcoal. The dry heat of the charcoal does a better job of browning the meat, and smoking wood is more effective in charcoal grills. But I use my gas grill's rotisserie all the time. It is so convenient.

I am a snob about cheap gas grills. It is expensive to make a gas grill that generates enough heat to be an effective rotisserie. (If the grill has a dedicated rotisserie burner, that's a great sign.) Don't expect a cheap, two burner grill to turn out good rotisserie.

Q: Why does my rotisserie roast have brown zebra stripes?

A: This is an oddity that I've noticed a few times myself, usually with wet brined food and my gas grill. The brown stripes are caused by drops of meat juices rolling around the outside of the roast. The juices leave a trail of browning behind them. Normally the brown trails spread out and cover the entire roast. But, sometimes they make trails that all the juices seem to follow. The result is dark brown stripes with pale stripes between them. If the roast cooks for long enough, the juices wander off the previous trails and fill in the stripes. But if the cooking time is short (Cornish game hens for example) the stripes do not have time to fill in. If this happens, don't worry about it. The roast tastes just as good, even with the striped browning.

ROTISSERIE CHICKEN

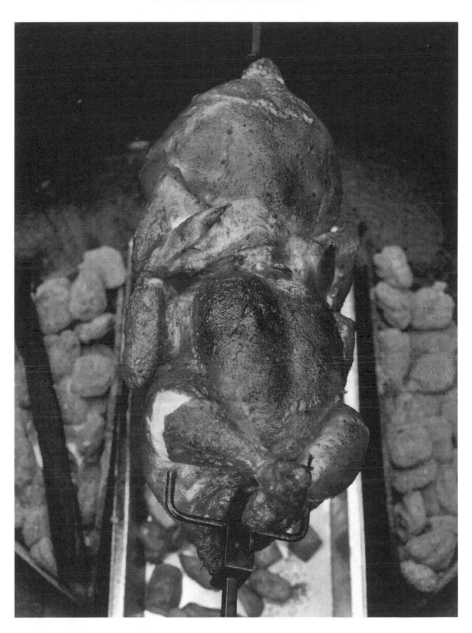

And this is how it all got started.

I bought my rotisserie specifically to make rotisserie chicken. My choice for a last supper would be a simple roast chicken with new potatoes and a side of green beans. I can make a good roast chicken in the oven, and a better one on the grill. Rotisserie grilling makes the best chicken I've ever had.

It seems like every grocery store in America sells rotisserie chicken. There's a reason for that - rotisserie chicken is delicious, and hard to screw up.

Another reason they all have rotisserie chicken? Psychological warfare. You've heard the advice: "Don't shop on an empty stomach?" My local grocery store has the rotisserie near the front door. The smell of roasted chicken greets me when I walk in with my cart, and it doesn't matter how long ago I ate...I'm hungry again.

Chicken cooking notes

Roasting a chicken is simple, but not easy. Breast meat dries out when cooked over 160°F, but legs don't get tender until 170°F to 180°F. Trussing the chicken helps by pushing the drumsticks out from the bird, exposing them to more heat and cooking them faster. On a rotisserie, the breast and legs reach the right cooking temperature at the same time.

Because of the breast meat, an instant read thermometer is an important tool when cooking chicken. You want to pull the chicken off the grill as close to 160°F as possible. Measure the temperature of the chicken in the thickest part of the breast. I go straight in from the front of the bird, a little to the side of the neck cavity.

All the recipes in this section double easily - a second bird takes the same amount of time. I rarely cook one chicken; the second bird gives me extra wings for my wife, and leftovers for the rest of the week. Chicken sandwiches, chicken noodle soup, chicken salad... If the spit is long enough you can cook three (or even four) chickens at the same time.

The timings are for a four pound chicken, known as a "broiler/fryer" at the store. Over indirect high heat (450°F), a 4 pound chicken takes about an hour to cook. Assume about 15 minutes per pound; a 3 1/2 pound bird is done in about 50 minutes, a 5 pound bird is done in 1 hour and 15 minutes.

Chicken with Basic Dry Brine

I make dry brined chicken more than all the other recipes in this cookbook combined. When I say "I love rotisserie chicken", I see this bird in my mind's eye.

I learned the dry brine technique from Judy Rodgers' Zuni Cafe Cookbook, where she called it pre-salting. It's a simple technique: salt and pepper a chicken, and let it rest in the refrigerator overnight. The salt penetrates deep into the meat, and the result is perfectly seasoned chicken with minimal effort.

This recipe does need advance planning, and some days I'm not that organized. It's OK to salt the chicken right before it goes on the grill; it won't be as deeply seasoned as the dry brine version, but it will still taste delicious.

Ingredients

- 1 (4 pound) chicken
- 1 tablespoon kosher salt
- 1 teaspoon freshly ground black pepper
- Fist sized chunk of smoking wood (or 1 cup wood chips)

Directions

1. Dry brine the chicken

Season the chicken with the salt and pepper, inside and out. Gently work your fingers under the skin on the breast, then rub some of the salt and pepper directly onto the breast meat. Refrigerate for at least two hours, preferably overnight.

2. Truss and spit the chicken

One hour before cooking, remove the chicken from the refrigerator. Fold the wingtips underneath the wings, then truss the chicken. Skewer the chicken on the rotisserie spit, securing it with the spit forks. Let the chicken rest at room temperature while the grill pre-heats. Submerge the smoking wood in water and let it soak until the grill is ready.

3. Set up the grill for indirect high heat

Set the grill up for indirect high heat with the drip pan in the middle of the grill.

4. Rotisserie cook the chicken

Put the spit on the grill, start the motor spinning, and make sure the drip pan is centered beneath the chicken. Add the smoking wood to the fire, then close the lid and cook until the chicken reaches 160°F in the thickest part of the breast, about 1 hour.

5. Serve

Remove the chicken from the rotisserie spit and remove the twine trussing the chicken. Be careful - the spit and forks are blazing hot. Let the chicken rest for 15 minutes, then carve and serve.

Chicken With Spice Rub

Let's spice things up with a quick rub from the spice cabinet. Sprinkle it on heavily; you want a thick crust of spices on the chicken. Make sure to work some under the skin and directly onto the breast meat, and toss some inside cavity of the bird, especially on the inside of the thighs.

Smoked Spanish paprika used to be a specialty ingredient, but it is becoming more common. It adds an extra smoke flavor to the rub, which is useful on a gas grill where smoking wood doesn't work as well. Use regular paprika if you can't find smoked.

Ingredients

- 1 (4 pound) chicken

Spice Rub

- 1 tablespoon kosher salt
- 1 teaspoon freshly ground black pepper
- 2 teaspoons sweet paprika (or smoked Spanish paprika)
- 1 teaspoon garlic powder
- 1 teaspoon ground coriander
- 1/2 teaspoon ground cumin
- 1/4 teaspoon ground cayenne pepper (optional)
- Fist sized chunk of smoking wood (or 1 cup wood chips)

Directions

1. Season, truss and spit the chicken

Mix the spice rub ingredients in a small bowl. Sprinkle the chicken with the spice rub inside and out, patting it onto the chicken to help it stick. Gently work your fingers under the skin on the breast, then rub some of the spice mix directly onto the breast meat.

Fold the wingtips under the wings and truss the chicken. Skewer the chicken on the rotisserie spit, securing it with the spit forks. Let the chicken rest at room temperature while the grill pre-heats. Submerge the smoking wood in water and let it soak until the grill is ready.

2. Set up the grill for indirect high heat

Set the grill up for indirect high heat with the drip pan in the middle of the grill.

3. Rotisserie cook the chicken

Put the spit on the grill, start the motor spinning, and make sure the drip pan is centered beneath the chicken. Add the smoking wood to the fire, close the lid, and cook until the chicken reaches 160°F in the thickest part of the breast, about 1 hour.

4. Serve

Remove the chicken from the rotisserie spit and remove the twine trussing the chicken. Be careful - the spit and forks are blazing hot. Let the chicken rest for 15 minutes, then carve and serve.

Notes

- If you have the time, use the spice rub as a dry brine. Rub the chicken the day before, and let it rest in the refrigerator overnight.

- The spices in this rub may burn. If you are cooking on a gas grill, check the roast after a half an hour. If the chicken is browning well, turn the heat down to medium for the rest of the cooking time.

Chicken With Fresh Herb Rub

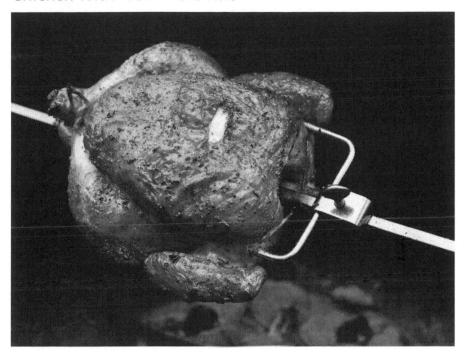

This rub is a little bit of every herb in a grocery store "poultry pack". You don't need these exact herbs; mince one tablespoon of whatever fresh herbs are on hand. In the summer, I make this herb rub from the thyme, rosemary, and parsley bushes that grow in my back yard.

If you do use a different blend of herbs, go easy on rosemary. It has a strong pine flavor that can overwhelm chicken. Don't add more than one teaspoon of rosemary to the rub.

Ingredients

- 1 (4 pound) chicken

Herb Rub

- 1 tablespoon kosher salt
- 1 teaspoon freshly ground black pepper
- 2 teaspoons minced thyme
- 1/2 teaspoon minced rosemary
- 1/2 teaspoon minced oregano
- 1/2 teaspoon minced sage

Directions

1. Season, truss and spit the chicken

Mix the herb rub ingredients in a small bowl. Rub the chicken with the herbs inside and out. Gently work your fingers under the skin on the breast, then rub some of the herb mix directly onto the breast meat. Fold the wingtips under the wings and truss the chicken. Skewer the chicken on the rotisserie spit, securing it with the spit forks. Let the chicken rest at room temperature until it is time to grill.

2. Set up the grill for indirect high heat

Set the grill up for indirect high heat with the drip pan in the middle of the grill.

3. Rotisserie cook the chicken

Put the spit on the grill, start the motor spinning, and make sure the drip pan is centered beneath the chicken. Close the lid and cook until the chicken reaches 160°F in the thickest part of the breast, about 1 hour.

4. Serve

Remove the chicken from the rotisserie spit and remove the twine trussing the chicken. Be careful - the spit and forks are blazing hot. Let the chicken rest for 15 minutes, then carve and serve.

Barbecued Chicken

I love real barbecue, pork shoulder and beef brisket cooked low and slow. But I'm a Northerner, so when I think of barbecued chicken, I think of thick, sweet, tomato based barbecue sauce.

The problem is, barbecue sauce burns. The high heat of the grill and the sugar in the sauce are a bad combination. I want a glaze on my chicken, not charred carbon. I wait until the last fifteen minutes of cooking, then brush on the sauce in a few layers. This is just enough time to caramelize the sugar in the sauce and thicken it into a tight glaze.

Equipment

- Sauce brush

Ingredients

- 1 (4 pound) chicken

Barbecue Sauce

- 1 cup ketchup
- 1/4 cup honey
- 1/4 cup cider vinegar
- 1 tablespoon Worcestershire sauce
- 1 tablespoon soy sauce
- 1 tablespoon hot sauce

Barbecue Rub

- 1 tablespoon kosher salt
- 1 teaspoon freshly ground black pepper
- 2 teaspoons paprika
- 2 teaspoons brown sugar
- 2 teaspoons chili powder
- 1/2 teaspoon garlic powder
- 1/2 teaspoon onion powder
- 1/2 teaspoon dried thyme

- Fist sized chunk of smoking wood (or 1 cup wood chips)

Directions

1. Season, truss and spit the chicken

Whisk the barbecue sauce ingredients in a bowl, then set aside.

Mix the barbecue rub ingredients in a small bowl. Break up any clumps of brown sugar until it is completely mixed with the other spices. Sprinkle the chicken with the barbecue rub inside and out, patting it onto the chicken to help it stick. Gently work your fingers under the skin on the breast, then rub some of the barbecue rub directly onto the breast meat.

Fold the wingtips under the wings and truss the chicken. Skewer the chicken on the rotisserie spit, securing it with the spit forks. Let the chicken rest at room temperature until it is time to grill. Submerge the smoking wood in water and let it soak until the grill is ready.

2. Set up the grill for indirect high heat

Set the grill up for indirect high heat with the drip pan in the middle of the grill.

3. Rotisserie cook the chicken

Put the spit on the grill, start the motor spinning, and make sure the drip pan is centered beneath the chicken. Add the smoking wood to the fire, then close the lid and cook until the chicken reaches 160°F in the thickest part of the breast, about 1 hour. During the last 15 minutes of cooking, brush the chicken with the barbecue sauce every five minutes.

4. Serve

Remove the chicken from the rotisserie spit and remove the twine trussing the chicken. Be careful - the spit and forks are blazing hot. Let the chicken rest for 15 minutes, then carve and serve, passing the remaining barbecue sauce at the table.

Notes

- If you have the time, use the barbecue rub as a dry brine. Rub the chicken the day before, and let it rest in the refrigerator overnight.

- I make large batches of the rub and barbecue sauce. The rub keeps for about a year in the pantry, and the sauce keeps for a couple of months in the refrigerator.

Chicken Teriyaki

The Japanese know grilled chicken. At yakitori restaurants, every part of the chicken is cut into bite sized cubes, stuck on bamboo skewers, and grilled over a charcoal fire.

*I do mean every part; the only thing they don't serve are the feathers.

In this recipe, I'm making those bite sized skewers a little bigger - with a whole chicken on a spit.

Teriyaki sauce has four ingredients, simmered until thick: soy sauce, honey (or sugar), mirin, and ginger. You can buy bottled teriyaki sauce, but making your own is easy and tastes better. The hardest part is finding mirin, the sweet rice wine that gives teriyaki sauce its unique flavor. Check the international aisle of your local grocery store. If you strike out there, and you live in a medium to large sized city, search out your local Asian market. They are sure to have it.

*Of course, if you don't have a local Asian market, there's always the internet.

Equipment

- Sauce brush

Ingredients

- 1 (4 pound) chicken
- 1 tablespoon kosher salt

Teriyaki Sauce

- 1/4 cup soy sauce
- 1/4 cup mirin (Japanese sweet rice wine)
- 1/4 cup honey (or sugar)
- 1/4 inch slice of ginger, smashed

Directions

1. Season, truss and spit the chicken

Season the chicken with the salt, inside and out. Gently work your fingers under the skin on the breast, then rub some of the salt directly onto the breast meat. Fold the wingtips under the wings and truss the chicken. Skewer the chicken on the rotisserie spit, securing it with the spit forks. Let the chicken rest at room temperature until it is time to grill.

2. Set up the grill for indirect high heat

Set the grill up for indirect high heat with the drip pan in the middle of the grill.

3. Make the teriyaki sauce

While the grill is preheating, combine the soy sauce, mirin, honey, and ginger in a saucepan. Bring to a boil over medium-high heat, stirring often, then decrease the heat to low and simmer for 10 minutes, until the liquid is reduced by half.

4. Rotisserie cook the chicken

Put the spit on the grill, start the motor spinning, and make sure the drip pan is centered beneath the chicken. Close the lid and cook until the chicken reaches 160°F in the thickest part of the breast, about 1 hour. During the last 15 minutes of cooking, brush the chicken with the teriyaki sauce every five minutes.

5. Serve

Remove the chicken from the rotisserie spit and transfer to a platter. Be careful - the spit and forks are blazing hot. Remove the trussing twine, then brush the chicken one last time with the teriyaki sauce. Let the chicken rest for 15 minutes, then carve and serve, passing any remaining teriyaki sauce at the table.

Chicken with Mustard and Herbes De Provence

Julia Child taught me about Poulet a la Diable, a French bistro classic. Brush a mix of Dijon mustard and herbs on a chicken, and it turns into a spicy browned crust.

Your high school French isn't failing you. This is "Chicken of the Devil". Scary, right? Spicy mustard is the traditional French way to kick up the heat.

Ingredients

- 1 (4 pound) chicken

Mustard paste

- 1/4 cup Dijon mustard
- 1 tablespoon kosher salt
- 1 tablespoon Herbes de Provence
- 1 teaspoon freshly ground black pepper

Directions

1. Dry brine the chicken

Mix the mustard paste ingredients in a small bowl. Rub the chicken with the mustard paste, inside and out. Gently work your fingers under the skin on the breast, then rub some of the paste directly onto the breast meat. Refrigerate for at least two hours, preferably overnight.

2. Truss and spit the chicken

One hour before cooking, remove the chicken from the refrigerator. Fold the wingtips under the wings and truss the chicken. Skewer the chicken on the rotisserie spit, securing it with the spit forks. Let the chicken rest at room temperature until it is time to grill.

3. Set up the grill for indirect high heat

Set the grill up for indirect high heat with the drip pan in the middle of the grill.

4. Rotisserie cook the chicken

Put the spit on the grill, start the motor spinning, and make sure the drip pan is centered beneath the chicken. Close the lid and cook until the chicken reaches 160°F in the thickest part of the breast, about 1 hour.

5. Serve

Remove the chicken from the rotisserie spit and remove the twine trussing the chicken. Be careful - the spit and forks are blazing hot. Let the chicken rest for 15 minutes, then carve and serve.

Notes

- Don't have time to dry brine? That's OK. The mustard crust has a lot of flavor; spread it on right before cooking.

- Want more heat in your Chicken of the Devil? Use horseradish Dijon instead of regular Dijon mustard.

Chicken with Brown Sugar, Garlic, and Bay Wet Brine

I use this technique when I'm cooking a chicken the day I bought it. I prefer dry brines, but only if I rest the chicken overnight. A wet brine does a better job of seasoning if I only have four hours.

The good news is, cooking a wet brined chicken on the rotisserie solves a lot of the problems with wet brines. The extra browning from the rotisserie counters the extra water absorbed by the brine, and the result is the best wet brined chicken ever.

Ingredients

- 1 (4 pound) chicken

Brine

- 2 quarts cold water
- 1/2 cup table salt (or 1 cup kosher salt)
- 1/4 cup brown sugar
- 1/2 head of garlic (6 to 8 cloves), skin on, crushed
- 3 bay leaves, crumbled
- 1 tablespoon peppercorns, crushed or coarsely ground (use the largest setting on your pepper mill)

Directions

1. Brine the chicken

Combine the brine ingredients in large container, and stir until the salt and sugar dissolve. Submerge the chicken in the brine. Store in the refrigerator for at least one hour, preferably four hours, no longer than eight hours.

2. Truss and spit the chicken

Remove the chicken from the brine and pat dry with paper towels, picking off any pieces of bay leaves or garlic that stick to the chicken. Fold the wingtips underneath the wings, then truss the chicken. Skewer the chicken on the rotisserie spit, securing it with the spit forks. Let the chicken rest at room temperature until it is time to grill.

3. Set up the grill for indirect high heat

Set the grill up for indirect high heat with the drip pan in the middle of the grill.

4. Rotisserie cook the chicken

Put the spit on the grill, start the motor spinning, and make sure the drip pan is centered beneath the chicken. Close the lid and cook until the chicken reaches 160°F in the thickest part of the breast, about 1 hour.

5. Serve

Remove the chicken from the rotisserie spit and remove the twine trussing the chicken. Be careful - the spit and forks are blazing hot. Let the chicken rest for 15 minutes, then carve and serve.

Notes

- Brining container - I use eight quart food service containers, which are the perfect size for two chickens back to back. I also use my big pasta pot for brining, and once used a deep pot that barely fit the chicken. All you need is a container deep enough to submerge the chicken that will also fit in your refrigerator. A lid that seals is a bonus, because it will make it harder to spill the brine when you move the chicken around.

Chicken with Mediterranean Marinade

This chicken could be from Spain or the south of France, Italy or Greece, Sicily or Lebanon. It has the flavors of the Mediterranean - olive oil, lemon, garlic, and thyme. It makes me imagine sunny days near a brilliant blue sea.

The marinade is really a brinerade. It has enough salt to get the brining effect, while the other ingredients season the outside of the bird.

Don't marinate for more than four hours. The lemon juice adds a lot of acid to the marinade, and it will start to cook the outside of the meat.

Ingredients

- 1 (4 pound) chicken

Marinade

- Juice and zest of 1 lemon, rind reserved for stuffing
- 1 tablespoon kosher salt
- 2 tablespoons fresh thyme leaves (or 1 tablespoon dried thyme)
- 1 teaspoon honey
- 4 garlic cloves, minced or pressed through a garlic press
- 1/4 cup Extra Virgin Olive Oil

Directions

1. Marinate the chicken

Mix the marinade ingredients in a gallon zip-top bag. Put the chicken in the bag and massage the marinade over the chicken through the plastic. Squeeze the air out of the bag, seal, and put the bagged chicken in a baking dish. Store in the refrigerator for at least one hour, preferably four hours, turning occasionally.

2. Truss and spit the chicken

One hour before cooking, remove the chicken from the refrigerator. Right before setting up the grill, remove the chicken from the bag and wipe off any excess marinade. Stuff the cavity of the chicken with the squeezed lemon rind. Fold the wingtips under the wings and truss the chicken. Skewer the chicken on the rotisserie spit, securing it with the spit forks. Let the chicken rest at room temperature until it is time to grill.

3. Set up the grill for indirect high heat

Set the grill up for indirect high heat with the drip pan in the middle of the grill.

4. Rotisserie cook the chicken

Put the spit on the grill, start the motor spinning, and make sure the drip pan is centered beneath the chicken. Close the lid and cook until the chicken reaches 160°F in the thickest part of the breast, about 1 hour.

5. Serve

Remove the chicken from the rotisserie spit and remove the twine trussing the chicken. Be careful - the spit and forks are blazing hot. Let the chicken rest for 15 minutes, then carve and serve.

Chicken Tandoori

Tandoori chicken is the showpiece of India's tandoor cooking. A Tandoor is a large clay oven, shaped like a bottle, with a layer of coals on the bottom. Skinless chicken is coated with yogurt marinade, skewered on a long spit, and lowered into the tandoor. The point of the spit rests in the coals; the chicken grills from the heat of the fire, and bakes in the heat radiating from the thick clay walls of the oven.

Tandoori cooking is very close to rotisserie cooking; both have a long spit and cook over coals. All that's missing is the spinning rotisserie motor.

It is traditional to remove the chicken's skin before applying the yogurt marinade. The yogurt protects the chicken meat from drying out in the heat of the grill, just like the skin would. Also, the skin won't get crisp under the layer of yogurt. Removing the skin is tricky, but worth the extra work.

Except for the skin on the wings. There the skin really doesn't want to peel off. I leave the skin on the wings, because it's a lot of work to remove it. I've seen some recipes that solve the problem by cutting the wings off the bird entirely. Either way, don't worry about the wings.

Once the chicken is skinned, cut deep slashes down to the bone every couple of inches. This is another tradition; it creates more surface area for the marinade to cover, and helps the chicken cook quicker.

Ingredients

- 1 (4 pound) chicken

Tandoori marinade

- 1 cup plain yogurt
- Juice of 1 lemon
- 1 tablespoon kosher salt
- 2 teaspoons ground cumin
- 2 teaspoons ground coriander
- 2 teaspoons paprika
- 1/2 teaspoon ground turmeric
- 1/2 teaspoon fresh ground black pepper
- 1/4 teaspoon cayenne pepper
- 2 cloves garlic, minced or pressed through a garlic press
- 1/2 inch piece of ginger, minced
- 1/2 teaspoon red food coloring (optional)

Garnish

- Minced cilantro leaves

Directions

1. Marinate the chicken

Mix the tandoori marinade ingredients in a gallon zip top bag until completely combined.

Next, skin the chicken. Cut through the skin along the backbone, then grab the skin with a paper towel and pull and cut the skin away from the chicken. (Don't worry about the skin on the wings, unless you're a perfectionist.)

Slash the breast down to the bone in two places, slash the thigh and drumstick once each, and slash where the drumstick and thigh meet. Put the chicken in the bag and massage the marinade over the chicken through the plastic. Squeeze the air out of the bag, seal, and put the bagged chicken in a baking dish. Store in the refrigerator for at least one hour, preferably four hours, turning occasionally.

2. Truss and spit the chicken

One hour before cooking, remove the chicken from the refrigerator. Just before cooking, remove the chicken from the bag and wipe off any excess marinade. Fold the wingtips under the wings and truss the chicken. Skewer the chicken on the rotisserie spit, securing it with the spit forks. Let the chicken rest at room temperature until it is time to grill.

3. Set up the grill for indirect high heat

Set the grill up for indirect high heat with the drip pan in the middle of the grill.

4. Rotisserie cook the chicken

Put the spit on the grill, start the motor spinning, and make sure the drip pan is centered beneath the chicken. Close the lid and cook the chicken for 30 minutes. Turn the heat down to medium and cook the chicken until it reaches 160°F in the thickest part of the breast, about another 30 minutes, for 1 hour of total cooking time. (If you are cooking with charcoal, don't worry about turning the heat down. The heat will come down naturally as the bird cooks.)

5. Serve

Remove the chicken from the rotisserie spit and remove the twine trussing the chicken. Be careful - the spit and forks are blazing hot. Let the chicken rest for 15 minutes, then carve and serve.

Notes

- This is a messy recipe; working with the tandoori marinade is like making a mud pie - thick and gloopy. (Is gloopy a word? I don't care. In this case, it fits.) If you're the kind of person who doesn't like mud pies, this recipe is not for you.

- To double this recipe, use two separate bags, one per chicken.

Chicken Legs Brazilian Churrasco Style

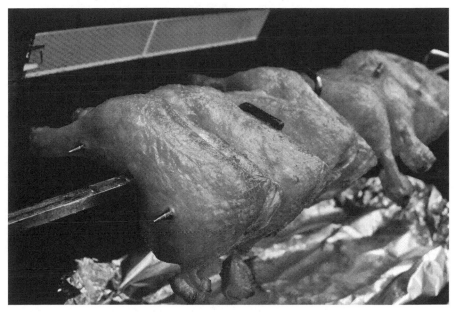

Churrascarias are Brazil's steakhouses. They specialize in Churrasco, skewers of meat roasted over an open fire. It is mostly beef, but there are some poultry skewers, like these chicken legs. The meat is served "rodizio style". Waiters bring a stream of skewers to your table until you beg for mercy.

I loved it. Once I recovered from the meat blizzard, I had to duplicate the recipes at home.

Churrasco chicken legs are simple - legs skewered on a spit, sprinkled with rock salt, and cooked on the rotisserie. The chicken skin is so crisp it seems deep fried. In a way, it is fried; the legs roast in their own fat on the rotisserie.

I added a basting sauce to give them a little extra flavor, but that's optional.

The only tricky part is securing the legs. They need to be skewered in two places, or they will work loose and not spin with the spit. I can fit two legs per fork, so I need four spit forks for eight legs. If your rotisserie came with two forks, get in touch with the manufacturer to buy an extra set.

Equipment

- 4 rotisserie forks

Ingredients

- 8 chicken legs
- 4 teaspoons kosher salt

Basting sauce

- Juice of 3 limes
- 3 cloves garlic, minced
- 1/8 teaspoon (a pinch) kosher salt

Directions

1. Spit and salt the chicken

Skewer the legs on the spit, two legs for each spit fork. Skewer each leg at a 45 degree angle, with the spit running through the bend of the leg, one spit fork prong in the thigh, and the other in the drumstick. Try to keep a gap between the legs so they brown properly. Salt the legs heavily, then rest at room temperature while pre-heating the grill.

2. Basting sauce

Mix the basting sauce in a small bowl until the salt dissolves.

3. Set up the grill for indirect high heat

Set the grill up for indirect high heat with the drip pan in the middle of the grill.

4. Rotisserie cook the chicken

Put the spit on the grill, start the motor spinning, and make sure the drip pan is centered beneath the chicken. Close the lid and cook until the chicken skin is crispy and the legs reach 180°F in the thickest part of the thigh, about 45 minutes. During the last 15 minutes of cooking, brush the chicken with the basting sauce every five minutes.

5. Serve

Remove the chicken from the rotisserie spit and transfer to a platter. Be careful - the spit and forks are blazing hot. Let the chicken rest for 10 minutes before serving.

Skewering two chicken legs on a single fork

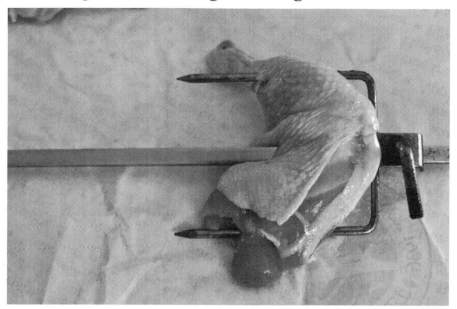

First leg on the fork

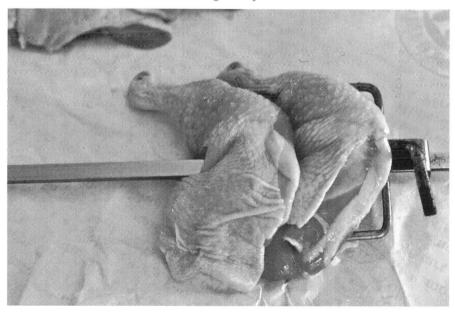

Second leg on the fork

Chicken is not the only bird you should grill on the rotisserie. From tiny Cornish game hens up to huge turkeys, the rotisserie cooks them all to perfection.

Poultry cooking notes

Cornish hens are little chickens, not a different breed of bird. Because they are small chickens, they cook the same way, just not quite as long.

Turkey is tricky. We have to take special measures to keep the extra lean white meat moist, while still cooking the legs through. Bank the fire entirely on the leg side of the bird, and cook the breast to no more than 155°F. In fact, if you're only cooking a turkey breast, and don't have to worry about the legs, pull it at 150°F to get it as juicy as possible.

Duck has a thick layer of fat between the skin and the meat, and we need to render as much of that fat as possible. The rotisserie is perfect for this, crisping up the skin and letting the fat drop into the drip pan. (Where you should have some drip pan potatoes cooking - duck fat potatoes are amazing.)

Cornish Hens with Tex-Mex Rub, Stuffed with Lime and Herbs

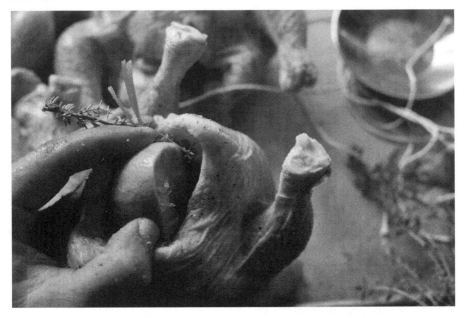

I love Cornish hens; they are cute, tiny chickens. Half of a hen is a perfect adult sized serving. You get a taste of everything - a crispy wing, tender white meat in the breast, a juicy thigh, and a drumstick to gnaw on.

Big eaters will need an entire hen for themselves. Maybe a hen and a half, once they find out how good these little chickens are.

This recipe has a simple southwestern rub, with salt, pepper, and a backbone of ancho chili powder. Cornish hens cook through in a little over a half an hour, making it hard to brown the skin before they come off the grill. A spice rub helps by giving the birds a layer of seasoning that toasts quickly. I also stuff the hens with lime and herbs to perfume the meat from the inside. The result is complete seasoning - spicy and crispy on the outside, herbs and citrus on the inside.

Ingredients

- 4 (1.75 pound) Cornish game hens
- 6 teaspoons kosher salt
- 2 teaspoons freshly ground black pepper
- 2 teaspoons ancho chili powder
- 2 limes, halved
- 4 thyme sprigs
- 4 cilantro sprigs

- Fist sized chunk of smoking wood (or 1 cup wood chips)

Directions

1. Season the hens

Up to two days before cooking: mix the salt, pepper, and ancho chili powder in a small bowl. Season the hens with the spice mix inside and out. Gently work your fingers under the skin on the breast, then rub some of the spice mix directly onto the breast meat. Stuff the cavity of each hen with a lime half, thyme sprig, and cilantro sprig. Refrigerate for at least two hours, preferably overnight.

2. Truss and spit the hens

One hour before cooking, remove the hens from the refrigerator. Fold the wingtips underneath the wings, then truss the hens. Skewer the hens on the rotisserie spit, securing them with the spit forks. Let the hens rest at room temperature until it is time to grill. Submerge the smoking wood in water and let it soak until the grill is ready.

3. Set up the grill for indirect high heat

Set the grill up for indirect high heat with the drip pan in the middle of the grill.

4. Rotisserie cook the hens

Put the spit on the grill, start the motor spinning, and make sure the drip pan is centered beneath the hens. Add the smoking wood to the fire, close the lid and cook until the hens reach 160°F in the thickest part of the breast, about 35 minutes.

5. Serve

Remove the hens from the rotisserie spit and remove the twine trussing the hens. Be careful - the spit and forks are blazing hot. Let the hens rest for 15 minutes, then split each hen down the middle. Discarding the lime and herbs that were in the cavity and serve.

Cornish Hens with Brown and Wild Rice Stuffing

This recipe has sentimental value. My grandfather's favorite meal was little chickens with rice stuffing. Every summer, he would travel in from Milwaukee to help us with a home improvement project. We would always have a dinner of stuffed Cornish hens while he was in town.

*Vrobel men communicate through home improvement. Want to spend time with Dad? Help him shingle the roof. Want my brother to visit? Ask him to help build a deck. Want to see the new house? Great, we've got everything boxed up, come load the moving van. Other than that, you'll find us standing around the grill with a tasty beverage, not saying much. Hey, we're guys. That's how we're wired.

In honor of my grandfather, I wanted to make stuffed little chickens on the rotisserie. It wasn't easy. Stuffing a bird usually results in undercooked stuffing (a health hazard) or dry, overcooked meat (a tragedy). The trick is to cook the stuffing to 170°F, then carefully spoon the hot stuffing into the birds right before trussing. By the time the birds are done, the stuffing has re-heated to 160°F, and everything is ready to serve.

Ingredients

- 4 (1.75 pound) Cornish game hens
- 6 teaspoons kosher salt (about 1 1/2 teaspoons per hen)
- 2 teaspoons freshly ground black pepper (about 1/2 teaspoon per hen)

Stuffing

- 2 cups cooked brown and wild rice blend
- 4 tablespoons butter
- 1 large onion, minced
- 1/2 teaspoon kosher salt
- 2 cloves garlic, minced
- 1 teaspoon minced fresh sage
- 1/2 cup raisins
- Zest of 1 lemon
- Salt and pepper for seasoning

Directions

1. Make the stuffing

Cook the brown and wild rice blend according to the package directions. (The rice can be cooked up to a day ahead of time and stored in the refrigerator). Heat the butter in a large skillet over medium-high heat until it stops foaming. Add the onion and 1/2 teaspoon of kosher salt and saute until the onion softens, about 5 minutes. Add the garlic and sage, and cook for 1 minute, or until you smell garlic. Stir in the brown and wild rice, raisins, and lemon zest. Taste the stuffing and season with more salt and pepper if necessary. Turn off the heat under the stuffing, cover the pan, and let it rest until it is time to stuff the birds.

2. Season the hens

Season the hens with salt and pepper, inside and out. Gently work your fingers under the skin on the breast, then rub some of the salt and pepper directly onto the breast meat.

3. Set up the grill for indirect high heat

Set the grill up for indirect high heat with the drip pan in the middle of the grill.

4. Stuff, truss and spit the hens

While the grill is pre-heating: Re-heat the pan of stuffing until it reaches an internal temperature of 170°F, stirring often. Loosely fill the cavity of each bird with stuffing, about 1/2 cup per bird. Fold the wingtips underneath the wings, then truss the hens. Skewer the hens on the rotisserie spit, and secure the hens with the spit forks, squeezing them together to hold the stuffing in.

5. Rotisserie cook the hens

Put the spit on the grill, start the motor spinning, and make sure the drip pan is centered beneath the hens. Close the lid and cook until the hens reach 160°F in the thickest part of the breast and the stuffing returns to 160°F, about 45 minutes.

6. Serve

Remove the hens from the rotisserie spit and remove the twine trussing the hens. Be careful - the spit and forks are blazing hot. Let the hens rest for 15 minutes, then split the hens. Scoop the stuffing onto plates, set a half hen on each plate, and serve.

Notes

- Extra stuffing: If you want to extra stuffing to serve at the table, double the stuffing recipe. Don't get raw Cornish hen juices in the extra stuffing; reserve two cups of the stuffing for the birds, then reheat the rest just before serving.

- Unlike my other Cornish hen recipes, I squeeze stuffed hens together on the spit, regardless of how much room I have. This holds the stuffing in the birds. The one on the end will lose a little bit of stuffing, so make sure to tie the drumsticks tight over the cavity when you are trussing it. That said, you are going to lose some of the stuffing while the hens spin; there should still be enough in the birds for everyone to have some as a side dish.

Cornish Hens with Thai Marinade

The combination of hot, sour, salty and sweet flavors define Thai cooking. Chili paste gives me the heat; lime juice is the traditional sour flavor in Thailand. Soy sauce provides the salty flavor, and is an effective base for marinades. Soy protein coats the outside of the hens and helps with browning, while the salt in soy sauce turns the marinade into a brine.

*Have I pounded home the brining effect yet? Sorry, but it is one of the key techniques to seasoning food.

Unfortunately, the sweet part doesn't work well on the rotisserie. Too much sugar makes the marinade burn in the heat of the grill. I had to cut way back on the sugar to get it to work on the rotisserie.

Ingredients

- 4 (1.75 pound) Cornish game hens

Marinade

- 4 cloves garlic, peeled
- 1 cup tightly packed leaves and stems of cilantro (I grab half a bunch from my grocery store)
- 2 teaspoons coriander seeds

- 1 cup soy sauce
- Juice of 1 lime
- 1/2 cup peanut oil
- 1 tablespoon Asian chili paste
- 1 teaspoon brown sugar

Directions

1. Marinate the hens

Drop the garlic cloves in a running food processor or blender, and process until completely minced. Add the cilantro and coriander, then pulse until the cilantro is minced. Scrape down the sides of the food processor and add the soy sauce, lime juice, peanut oil, chili paste, and brown sugar. Run the processor for 15 seconds to mix. Split the marinade between two gallon zip top bags and put two hens in each bag. Massage the marinade over the hens through the plastic. Squeeze the air out of the bags, seal, and put the bagged hens in a baking dish. Store in the refrigerator for at least one hour, preferably four hours, turning occasionally.

2. Truss and spit the hens

Remove the hens from the marinade, letting any excess drip off, and pat dry with paper towels. Fold the wingtips underneath the wings and truss the hens. Skewer the hens on the rotisserie spit, securing with the spit forks. Let the hens rest at room temperature until it is time to grill.

3. Set up the grill for indirect high heat

Set the grill up for indirect high heat with the drip pan in the middle of the grill.

4. Rotisserie cook the hens

Put the spit on the grill, start the motor spinning, and make sure the drip pan is centered beneath the hens. Close the lid and cook until the hens reach 160°F in the thickest part of the breast, about 35 minutes.

5. Serve

Remove the hens from the rotisserie spit and remove the twine trussing the hens. Be careful - the spit and forks are blazing hot. Let the hens rest for 15 minutes, then split and serve.

Notes

- No blender or food processor? Mince the garlic and cilantro, crush the coriander seed, and whisk everything together until well mixed.

- I like Huy Fong brand Sambal Oelek chili paste. You'll find it in the international aisle of your grocery store, right next to the Sriracha. (The same company makes both Sriracha and Sambal Oelek.) If you can't find chili paste, substitute a teaspoon of hot red pepper flakes.

Turkey with Basic Dry Brine

Everyone wants Thanksgiving dinner to be the Norman Rockwell picture of plenty, with a huge, bronzed bird at the center of the table.

The problem is, a whole turkey is tough to cook properly. The lean breast meat needs to be cooked as little as possible; every degree over 130°F pushes more juices out of the white meat; if the breast cooks past 165°F it will be very dry. But the tough turkey legs need to be well done, at least 170°F, to break down the connective tissue in the dark meat and make them tender.

And then there's the matter of safety. The United States Department of Agriculture has a time/temperature table for how long turkey must be cooked to kill salmonella. Turkey needs to be 150°F for at least 3.8 minutes, 155°F for 1.2 minutes, or 165°F for less than ten seconds to make sure salmonella is dead. The USDA recommends cooking turkey to 165°F; they don't trust home cooks or their thermometers, so they err on the side of absolute safety.

I trust my thermometer to keep me safe. When I cook a whole turkey, I aim for 155°F in the thickest part of the breast, and trust carry-over heat from the meat to keep it there for two minutes. 155°F gives me the best balance between juicy breast meat and tender dark meat. Trussing the turkey pushes the legs out, so they cook faster than the breast, and are closer to 170°F by the time the breast is done.

Ingredients

- 1 (12 to 14 pound) turkey

Dry brine

- 1/4 cup kosher salt
- 1 tablespoon minced fresh sage
- 1 tablespoon minced fresh thyme
- 1 teaspoon fresh ground black pepper

- Fist sized chunk of smoking wood (or 1 cup wood chips)

Directions

1: Dry brine the turkey

Mix the dry brine ingredients in a small bowl. Sprinkle the turkey with the dry brine, inside and out. Gently work your fingers under the skin on the breast, then rub some of the dry brine directly onto the breast meat. Refrigerate at least overnight, preferably two to three days. If dry brining more than a day in advance, cover the turkey with plastic wrap until the night before cooking, then remove the plastic wrap to let the skin dry out overnight.

2: Truss and spit the turkey

Two hours before cooking, remove the turkey from the refrigerator. Fold the wingtips underneath the wings, then truss the turkey. Skewer the turkey on the rotisserie spit, securing it with the spit forks. Let the turkey rest at room temperature until it is time to grill. Submerge the smoking wood in water and let it soak until the grill is ready.

3: Set up the grill for indirect medium heat

Set the grill up for indirect medium heat with the drip pan in the middle of the grill. Turkey is a special case - set all the heat on one side of the grill, facing the turkey legs. With a charcoal grill, make a U of charcoal, with the pan in the middle, and the breast facing the open part of the U. With a gas grill, if possible, turn on two burners on one side of the grill instead of one burner on each side.

4: Rotisserie cook the turkey

Put the spit on the grill, start the motor spinning, and make sure the drip pan is centered beneath the turkey. Add the smoking wood to the fire, close the lid and cook until the turkey reaches 155°F in the thickest part of the breast, about 2 1/2 hours.

5: Serve

Remove the turkey from the rotisserie spit and remove the twine trussing the turkey. Be very careful - the spit and forks are blazing hot. Let the turkey rest for 15 to 30 minutes, then carve and serve.

Notes

- Source for time/temperature information: USDA Food Safety and Inspection Service publication, Time-Temperature Tables For Cooking Ready-To-Eat Poultry Products

- Watch out for enhanced turkey. Turkey with "a ten percent added saline solution", or words to that effect on the package, have already been wet brined. This is how most frozen turkeys are sold; If you want to dry brine your turkey, get a fresh turkey that isn't already pumped up with salt water.

- If you have no choice but to buy an enhanced turkey, skip the dry brining, thaw the turkey, cut the salt back to 1 tablespoon of kosher salt, and rub the dry brine onto the turkey right before you truss it.

Turkey with Orange Spice Dry Brine

I used to wet brine my turkey every Thanksgiving. My favorite brine had apple cider, brown sugar, oranges, garlic, ginger, and cloves. The turkey smelled wonderful when it came off the grill, and tasted great.

Then I dry brined a turkey. After that, I never wet brined a turkey again. There is no comparison - the turkey flavor shines through with a dry brine.

I am a dry brine convert...but I kept thinking about the taste of that wet brine. I set out to make a dry brine based on those flavors, and succeeded beyond my wildest expectations. This is my favorite dry brine in the book. Don't save it for turkey - try it on any bird you want to cook on the rotisserie.

Ingredients

- 1 (12 to 14 pound) turkey

Dry brine

- 1/4 cup kosher salt
- Zest of 1 orange (save the orange rind, cut in half and wrapped in plastic wrap to stuff the turkey)
- 1 tablespoon grated fresh ginger (a 1 inch piece, grated)
- 4 cloves garlic, grated (about 2 teaspoons)
- 1 teaspoon brown sugar
- 1/2 teaspoon fresh ground black pepper
- 1/4 teaspoon ground cloves

- Fist sized chunk of smoking wood (or 1 cup wood chips)

Directions

1: Dry brine the turkey

Mix the dry brine ingredients in a small bowl. Sprinkle the turkey with the dry brine, inside and out. Gently work your fingers under the skin on the breast, then rub some of the dry brine directly onto the breast meat. Refrigerate at least overnight, preferably two to three days. If dry brining more than a day in advance, cover the turkey with plastic wrap until the night before cooking, then remove the plastic wrap to let the skin dry out overnight.

2: Truss and spit the turkey

Two hours before cooking, remove the turkey from the refrigerator. Put the orange rind halves in the cavity of the turkey. Fold the wingtips underneath the wings, then truss the turkey. Skewer the turkey on the rotisserie spit, securing it with the spit forks. Let the turkey rest at room temperature until it is time to grill. Submerge the smoking wood in water and let it soak until the grill is ready.

3: Set up the grill for indirect medium heat

Set the grill up for indirect medium heat with the drip pan in the middle of the grill. Turkey is a special case - set all the heat on one side of the grill, facing the turkey legs. With a charcoal grill, make a U of charcoal, with the pan in the middle, and the breast facing the open part of the U. With a gas grill, if possible, turn on two burners on one side of the grill instead of one burner on each side.

4: Rotisserie cook the turkey

Put the spit on the grill, start the motor spinning, and make sure the drip pan is centered beneath the turkey. Add the smoking wood to the fire, close the lid and cook until the turkey reaches 155°F in the thickest part of the breast, about 2 1/2 hours.

5: Serve

Remove the turkey from the rotisserie spit and remove the twine trussing the turkey. Be very careful - the spit and forks are blazing hot. Let the turkey rest for 15 to 30 minutes, then carve and serve.

Notes

- Watch out for enhanced turkey. Turkey with "a ten percent added saline solution", or words to that effect on the package, have already been wet brined. This is how most frozen turkeys are sold; If you want to dry brine your turkey, get a fresh turkey that isn't already pumped up with salt water.

- If you have no choice but to buy an enhanced turkey, skip the dry brining, thaw the turkey, cut the salt back to 1 tablespoon of kosher salt, and rub the dry brine onto the turkey right before you truss it.

Turkey with Cajun Spices

Deep fried turkey is a Cajun classic. I remember John Madden waving an impossibly crisp drumstick at halftime, and the memory makes me fire up my grill.

My grill? Not a fryer? Yes, I'm biased towards rotisserie turkey. I've seen too many online videos where the pot of oil boils over and the turkey fryer becomes the world's largest tiki torch.

In the original version, Cajun spices and melted butter are injected deep into the turkey with a massive syringe, and then the big bird is slowly lowered into a pot of boiling oil. This will impress the guests, and I'm not against showmanship, but the results aren't as good as a dry brined rotisserie turkey.

Because the turkey is not cooking in boiling oil, the spices can go on the outside of the bird. I gave up on injecting; my needlework was all over the place. Some of the turkey wound up with big veins of spices, while other parts would be completely unseasoned. Add some smoking wood (hickory or pecan are traditional), and the result is a bird that's even better than deep fried.

Ingredients

- 1 (12 to 14 pound) turkey

Dry brine

- 1/4 cup kosher salt
- 1 tablespoon paprika
- 1 tablespoon granulated garlic
- 1 1/2 teaspoons granulated onion
- 1 1/2 teaspoons fresh ground black pepper
- 1 1/2 teaspoons dried oregano
- 1 1/2 teaspoons dried thyme
- 1/2 teaspoon cayenne pepper

- Fist sized chunk of smoking wood (or 1 cup wood chips)

Directions

1: Dry brine the turkey

Mix the dry brine ingredients in a small bowl. Sprinkle the turkey with the dry brine, inside and out. Gently work your fingers under the skin on the breast, then rub some of the dry brine directly onto the breast meat. Refrigerate at least overnight, preferably two to three days. If dry brining more than a day in advance, cover the turkey with plastic wrap until the night before cooking, then remove the plastic wrap to let the skin dry out overnight.

2: Truss and spit the turkey

Two hours before cooking, remove the turkey from the refrigerator. Fold the wingtips underneath the wings, then truss the turkey. Skewer the turkey on the rotisserie spit, securing it with the spit forks. Let the turkey rest at room temperature until it is time to grill. Submerge the smoking wood in water and let it soak until the grill is ready.

3: Set up the grill for indirect medium heat

Set the grill up for indirect medium heat with the drip pan in the middle of the grill. Turkey is a special case - set all the heat on one side of the grill, facing the turkey legs. With a charcoal grill, make a U of charcoal, with the pan in the middle, and the breast facing the open part of the U. With a gas grill, if possible, turn on two burners on one side of the grill instead of one burner on each side.

4: Rotisserie cook the turkey

Put the spit on the grill, start the motor spinning, and make sure the drip pan is centered beneath the turkey. Add the smoking wood to the fire, close the lid, and cook until the turkey reaches 155°F in the thickest part of the breast, about 2 1/2 hours.

5: Serve

Remove the turkey from the rotisserie spit and remove the twine trussing the turkey. Be very careful - the spit and forks are blazing hot. Let the turkey rest for 15 to 30 minutes, then carve and serve.

Notes

- Watch out for enhanced turkey. Turkey with "a ten percent added saline solution", or words to that effect on the package, have already been wet brined. This is how most frozen turkeys are sold; If you want to dry brine your turkey, get a fresh turkey that isn't already pumped up with salt water.

- If you have no choice but to buy an enhanced turkey, skip the dry brining, thaw the turkey, cut the salt back to 1 tablespoon of kosher salt, and rub the dry brine onto the turkey right before you truss it.

Turkey Breast with Pastrami Rub

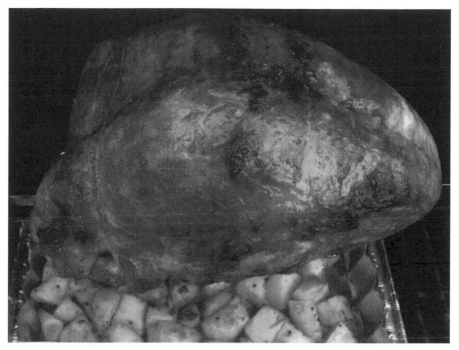

Turkey breast is easy to cook on the rotisserie. There's nothing to truss; the meat is firmly attached to the bird's ribcage, and there are no legs or wings flopping around. Just secure it with the spit forks and go.

Another turkey breast advantage: we only have to worry about the white meat. Without the bothersome legs, we can cook the breast to 150°F. The lower temperature means less juices are squeezed out of the meat, leaving the juiciest turkey breast you'll ever eat. The USDA says it needs to stay at 150°F for the 3.8 minutes to make sure any salmonella in the meat is killed. Carry-over heat will keep it there for at least ten minutes, so the turkey will be safe to eat.

See the Turkey with Basic Dry Brine recipe for a discussion on proper turkey cooking temperatures.

This isn't my brainstorm; Julia Child recommended it. She cut the legs away from the breast on her Thanksgiving turkey. That way, she could cook each the way it needs to be cooked. The breast would come out of the oven exactly when it was done, and the legs could stay in until the dark meat was nice and tender.

Ingredients

- 1 (7 pound) turkey breast

Spice rub

- 2 tablespoons kosher salt
- 1 tablespoon coarse ground black pepper
- 1 tablespoon coarse ground coriander seed
- 1 teaspoon brown sugar
- 4 cloves garlic, minced or pressed through a garlic press

Directions

1. Dry brine the turkey breast

Mix the spice rub ingredients in a small bowl. Rub the turkey breast with the spice rub, inside and out. Gently work your fingers under the skin on the breast, then rub some of the spice rub directly onto the breast meat. Refrigerate overnight.

2. Spit the turkey breast

Two hours before cooking, remove the turkey breast from the refrigerator. Skewer the breast on the rotisserie spit, securing it with the spit forks. Let the turkey rest at room temperature until it is time to grill.

3. Set up the grill for indirect medium heat

Set the grill up for indirect medium heat with the drip pan in the middle of the grill.

4. Rotisserie cook the turkey breast

Put the spit on the grill, start the motor spinning, and make sure the drip pan is centered beneath the turkey. Close the lid and cook until the turkey reaches 150°F in the thickest part of the breast, about 1 1/2 hours.

5. Serve

Remove the turkey breast from the rotisserie spit. Be very careful - the spit and forks are blazing hot. Let the turkey rest for 15 to 30 minutes, then carve and serve.

Notes

- Turkey breast is perfect for leftovers. Slice it thin and use it for sandwiches later in the week.

Duck with Maple Syrup Glaze

Roast duck is tricky, because of the thick layer of fat under its skin. If too much fat is left at the end of cooking, the duck meat will be greasy.

Cooking the duck on the rotisserie melts the fat better than any other cooking method I've used. Dry brining the duck also helps; the overnight rest in the refrigerator dehydrates the skin, helping it brown.

Duck fat isn't all bad - it tastes delicious. It bathes the meat and crisps up the skin. And then there are drip pan potatoes. Promise me you will make drip pan potatoes every time you cook a duck.

There will be a lot of rendered fat in the drip pan. Make sure you have a deep pan with no flames directly underneath. All it takes is one splatter of fat reaching the flames and you have a duck fat inferno. Also, be careful when you remove the drip pan. A foil pan buckled as I lifted it out of the grill, dumping duck fat all over the place. It took a week of burn-offs to get the grill to stop smoking.

If you have time, let the pan sit in the grill overnight. The fat will solidify as it cools, and you won't have to worry about spilling it and making a mess.

Ingredients

- 1 (5 1/2 pound) duck
- 4 teaspoons kosher salt
- 1 teaspoon freshly ground black pepper

Maple glaze

- 1/2 cup maple syrup
- Juice of 1 lemon

- Fist sized chunk of smoking wood (or 1 cup wood chips)

Directions

1. Dry brine the duck

Slash the skin on the duck in a 1/2 inch diamond pattern - cut one set of slashes 1/2 inch apart, then change directions and cut another set of slashes to form the diamonds. Cut through the skin and into the fat, but be careful not to slice into the meat. Season the duck with the salt and pepper, inside and out. Refrigerate, uncovered, for one to two days.

2. Truss and spit the duck

One hour before cooking, remove the duck from the refrigerator. Fold the wingtips underneath the wings, then truss the duck. Skewer the duck on the rotisserie spit, securing it with the spit forks. Let the duck rest at room temperature until it is time to grill. Submerge the smoking wood in water and let it soak until the grill is ready.

3. Make the glaze

Whisk the maple syrup and lemon juice in a small bowl.

4. Set up the grill for indirect high heat

Set the grill up for indirect high heat with the drip pan in the middle of the grill.

5. Rotisserie cook the duck

Put the spit on the grill, start the motor spinning, and make sure the drip pan is centered beneath the duck. Add the smoking wood to the fire, close the lid, and cook the duck until it reaches 180°F in the thickest part of the thigh, about 1 hour and 15 minutes. During the last 15 minutes of cooking, brush the duck with maple syrup every five minutes.

6. Serve

Remove the duck from the rotisserie spit and remove the twine trussing the duck. Be careful - the spit and forks are blazing hot. Brush with the maple glaze one last time. Let the duck rest for 15 minutes, then carve and serve.

Notes

- Use real maple syrup, not one of the cheap corn syrups made for pancakes. And, if you can find it, use grade B maple syrup; it's thicker than grade A syrup, with a stronger maple flavor.

Duck L'Orange

Duck L'Orange is a mainstay of white tablecloth French restaurants. In other words, it is old fashioned, and has fallen out of style. That's a shame, because fatty duck with tart and sweet orange flavors became a classic for a reason.

I don't have a cooking brigade to do the work, like a classic French chef, so I take some shortcuts. Instead of making a sauce out of duck stock and caramelized sugar, I use marmalade and fresh-squeezed orange juice. Then I add a couple more layers of orange flavor; orange zest is part of the dry brine, and I stuff the cavity of the duck with the squeezed orange rind.

Ingredients

- 1 (5 1/2 pound) duck
- 4 teaspoons kosher salt
- 1 teaspoon freshly ground black pepper
- Zest and squeezed rind of 1 orange (save the juice for the glaze)

Glaze

- Juice from 1 orange
- 1/2 cup orange marmalade
- 1/4 cup Madeira (or red wine)
- 1/2 teaspoon ground cayenne pepper

Directions

1. Dry brine the duck

Poke the skin on the duck all over with a paring knife, being careful not to pierce the meat. (I come at the duck from a very low angle, almost parallel to the skin, so I don't poke into the meat.) Season the duck with the salt, pepper, and orange zest, inside and out. Squeeze the juice out of the orange and set aside for later, then put the squeezed orange rind in the cavity of the duck. (Refrigerate the orange juice; we use it in the glaze.) Refrigerate, uncovered, for one to two days.

2. Truss and spit the duck

One hour before cooking, remove the duck from the refrigerator. Fold the wingtips underneath the wings, then truss the duck. Skewer the duck on the rotisserie spit, securing it with the spit forks. Let the duck rest at room temperature until it is time to grill.

3. Make the glaze

Heat the glaze ingredients over medium heat until the marmalade liquefies, then whisk to thoroughly mix the glaze.

4. Set up the grill for indirect high heat

Set the grill up for indirect high heat with the drip pan in the middle of the grill.

5. Rotisserie cook the duck

Put the spit on the grill, start the motor spinning, and make sure the drip pan is centered beneath the duck. Close the lid and cook the duck until it reaches 180°F in the thickest part of the thigh, about 1 hour and 15 minutes. During the last 15 minutes of cooking, brush the duck with marmalade glaze every five minutes.

6. Serve

Remove the duck from the rotisserie spit and remove the twine trussing the duck. Be careful - the spit and forks are blazing hot. Brush with the marmalade glaze one last time. Let the duck rest for 15 minutes, then carve and serve.

Peking Duck

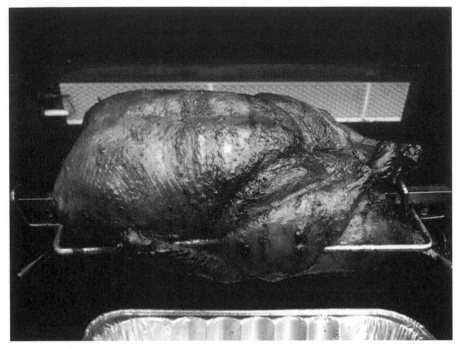

I've never been to China; I saw Beijing barbecued duck on a food travel show. Ducks are suspended from hooks over an open fire in a huge oven. The chef occasionally reaches in with a long pole and gives each duck a spin. The result is perfectly crisp duck, the kind displayed in Chinatown shop windows.

I only watch TV for the food shows. This far into the book, I don't think you're surprised.

The moment I saw the chef spin a duck, I had to try it on my rotisserie. I don't have an oven with open fire and hooks in the ceiling; I'm not that old school.

Here is my version of Peking (aka Beijing) duck, basted with a sweet glaze to add another layer of flavor to the crisp, crackling skin.

Ingredients

- 1 (5 1/2 pound) duck

Dry brine

- 4 teaspoons kosher salt

- 1 teaspoon freshly ground black pepper
- 2 cloves garlic, minced or pressed through a garlic press
- 1/2 inch piece of ginger, minced
- 1 teaspoon five spice powder

Stuffing

- 4 scallions, trimmed and cut into 1" pieces

Glaze

- 1/4 cup hoisin sauce
- 1/4 cup soy sauce
- 2 tablespoons honey
- 1 teaspoon sesame oil

Directions

1. Dry brine the duck

Poke the skin on the duck all over with a paring knife, being careful not to pierce the meat. (I come at the duck from a very low angle, almost parallel to the skin, so I don't poke into the meat.) Mix the dry brine ingredients in a small bowl. Season the duck with the dry brine inside and out. Stuff the scallions inside the duck. Refrigerate, uncovered, for one to two days.

2. Truss and spit the duck

One hour before cooking, remove the duck from the refrigerator. Fold the wingtips underneath the wings, then truss the duck. Skewer the duck on the rotisserie spit, securing it with the spit forks. Let the duck rest at room temperature until it is time to grill.

3. Make the glaze

Whisk the hoisin sauce, soy sauce, honey, and sesame oil in a small bowl.

4. Set up the grill for indirect high heat

Set the grill up for indirect high heat with the drip pan in the middle of the grill.

5. Rotisserie cook the duck

Put the spit on the grill, start the motor spinning, and make sure the drip pan is centered beneath the duck. Close the lid and cook the duck until it reaches 180°F in the thickest part of the thigh, about 1 hour and 15 minutes. During the last 15 minutes of cooking, brush the duck with hoisin glaze every five minutes.

6. Serve

Remove the duck from the rotisserie spit and remove the twine trussing the duck. Be careful - the spit and forks are blazing hot. Brush with the hoisin glaze one last time. Let the duck rest for 15 minutes, then carve and serve, passing any extra glaze on the side.

Notes

- Peking duck is served on top of thin rice pancakes, with a spoon of hoisin sauce and a sprinkling of slivered scallions. Warmed flour tortillas are an easy substitute for the rice pancakes.

Ribs and loins and butts, oh my.

A wise man once said: you can cook every part of the pig except for the oink. (He was right.) On the rotisserie you can make anything, from a lean pork loin, to a juicy pork shoulder, a sweet glazed ham, or crisp and tender ribs.

Pork cooking notes

Rotisserie pork technique depends entirely on the cut of meat.

- Pork loins are very lean, and dry out when they are overcooked. I cook them on the bone in a rack of pork, or tie two loin roasts together to thicken them up.

- Pork shoulder is probably my second favorite thing to rotisserie, right behind chicken. It is tough to overcook, and the tender meat surrounded by a crisp crust is a like the world's thickest piece of bacon.

- Pork ribs are like the shoulder, with the added advantage of bones to gnaw on. Sure, weaving ribs on a spit is inefficient, but the results are worth it.

- Ham is awesome on its own. Crisping it up on the rotisserie and coating it with a sweet glaze takes it to the next level.

This will sound familiar if you've read the turkey recipes, but: watch out for enhanced pork. Pork with "containing up to (some percent) of a solution" on the package has already been wet brined. Try to get natural pork, which you can flavor to your liking - once a pork has been enhanced, it won't be able to absorb any more brine. If you have no choice but to buy enhanced pork, skip the brining step, and go straight to any rubs or other seasonings in the recipe.

Pork Shoulder with Basic Wet Brine

Pork shoulder is my favorite cut of meat. It is a hard working set of muscles, full of tough and chewy tendons, and should not be cooked medium-rare. Those tendons start to melt into gelatin at a well done temperature of 160°F...but don't stop there. By the time the roast is cooked to 190°F, it is full of tender and juicy gelatin, and ready to shred with a fork.

This recipe uses a basic wet brine - just water, salt and sugar. Wet brining works better with pork than dry brining. I'm not sure why. Other meats seem to get watered down by the brine; pork tastes...porkier.

Is porkier a word? No? Oh well, you know what I mean.

Don't be fooled by the simplicity of this recipe. That hard working pork shoulder has a lot of flavor, and a simple brine builds on it to make a roast that is better than the sum of its ingredients.

Ingredients

- 1 (4 pound) boneless pork shoulder roast (aka Boston butt roast)

Brine

- 3 quarts water
- 1.5 cups kosher salt (3/4 cup table salt)
- 1/4 cup brown sugar

- Fist sized chunk of smoking wood (or 1 cup wood chips)

Directions

1. Brine the pork

Combine the brine ingredients in a large container and stir until the salt and sugar dissolve. Submerge the pork in the brine. Store in the refrigerator for four to eight hours.

2. Truss and spit the pork

One hour before cooking, remove the pork from the brine and pat dry with paper towels. Truss the pork roast, then skewer it on the rotisserie spit, securing it with the spit forks. Let the pork rest at room temperature until it is time to grill. Submerge the smoking wood in water and let it soak until the grill is ready.

3. Set up the grill for indirect medium heat

Set the grill up for indirect medium heat with the drip pan in the middle of the grill.

4. Rotisserie cook the pork

Put the spit on the grill, start the motor spinning, and make sure the drip pan is centered beneath the pork roast. Add the smoking wood to the fire, close the lid, and cook until the pork reaches 190°F in its thickest part, about 1 1/2 hours.

5. Serve

Remove the pork from the rotisserie spit and remove the twine trussing the roast. Be careful - the spit and forks are blazing hot. Let the pork rest for 15 minutes, then slice and serve.

Pork Shoulder with Italian Style Spice Rub

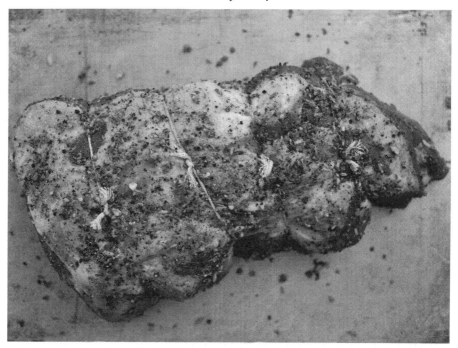

Porchetta is Italian roast pig. Not pork, pig. The whole pig is deboned, salted, and stuffed with a mix of fennel, rosemary, garlic and pepper. Then it is rolled, tied, and spit roasted over an open wood fire.

That whole hog roast inspires this simple version. I'm a cooking fanatic, but deboning a hog is beyond me. And my grill, big as it is, could never hold an entire pig.

I'm weakening, though. Maybe I can rent a giant spit roaster, and work on my butchering skills...

This is a recipe for a big pork shoulder - a six pounder will take a little longer to cook through than the other roasts in this book. That's OK - the extra time is worth it.

Ingredients

- 1 (6 pound) boneless pork shoulder roast (aka Boston butt roast)

Brine

- 3 quarts water
- 3/4 cup table salt (1.5 cups kosher salt)
- 1/4 cup brown sugar

Rub

- Zest of 1 lemon
- 4 cloves garlic, minced or pressed through a garlic press
- 1 tablespoon fennel seed, coarsely ground
- 1 tablespoon coriander seed, coarsely ground
- 1 tablespoon peppercorns, coarsely ground

Directions

1. Brine the pork

Combine the brine ingredients in a large container and stir until the salt and sugar dissolve. Submerge the pork in the brine. Store in the refrigerator for four to eight hours.

2. Rub, truss and spit the pork

One hour before cooking, remove the pork from the brine and pat dry with paper towels. Mix the rub ingredients in a small bowl, then spread the rub over the pork roast, working it into any natural seams in the meat with your fingers. Truss the pork, skewer it on the rotisserie spit, and secure with the spit forks. Let the pork rest at room temperature until it is time to grill.

3. Set up the grill for indirect medium heat

Set the grill up for indirect medium heat with the drip pan in the middle of the grill.

4. Rotisserie cook the pork

Put the spit on the grill, start the motor spinning, and make sure the drip pan is centered beneath the pork roast. Close the lid and cook until the pork reaches 190°F in its thickest part, about 2 1/2 hours.

5. Serve

Remove the pork from the rotisserie spit and remove the twine trussing the roast. Be careful - the spit and forks are blazing hot. Let the pork rest for 15 minutes, then slice and serve.

Pork Shoulder with Chinese Char Siu Glaze

Barbecued Pork, char siu, is a specialty of Cantonese rotisserie shops. Long strips of roasted pork, red from the char siu marinade, hang in the window of the shop. Chinese families use it over the course of a few days. First, it is served as the main course for dinner; then, leftover pork is diced and used to stuff buns or flavor stir fries.

Char siu marinade is a brine and a glaze, all wrapped into one. Salty soy sauce brines the pork; sweet honey and hoisin sauce form a sticky coating on the outside of the meat. I break the brine and the glaze apart, to keep the sugary glaze from burning during the pork shoulder's long cooking time.

Ingredients

- 1 (4 pound) boneless pork shoulder roast (aka Boston butt roast)

Brine

- 1 cup soy sauce
- 2 tablespoons hoisin sauce
- 4 cloves garlic, minced or pressed through a garlic press
- 2 inch piece of ginger, peeled and grated
- 2 tablespoons rice wine vinegar or dry sherry
- 1 tablespoon sesame oil

Glaze

- 1/4 cup honey
- 1/4 cup hoisin sauce
- 2 tablespoons soy sauce

Directions

1. Brine the pork

Mix the brine ingredients in a gallon zip top bag. Put the pork roast in the bag and massage with the brine through the plastic. Squeeze the air out of the bag, seal, and put the bagged roast in a baking dish. Store in the refrigerator for four to eight hours, turning occasionally.

2. Truss and spit the pork

One hour before cooking, remove the pork from the brine and pat dry with paper towels. Truss the roast, skewer it on the rotisserie spit, and secure it with the spit forks. Let the pork rest at room temperature until it is time to grill.

3. Make the glaze

Whisk the glaze ingredients in a small bowl.

4. Set up the grill for indirect medium heat

Set the grill up for indirect medium heat with the drip pan in the middle of the grill.

5. Rotisserie cook the pork

Put the spit on the grill, start the motor spinning, and make sure the drip pan is centered beneath the pork roast. Close the lid and cook the pork until it reaches 190°F in its thickest part, about 1 1/2 hours. During the last 15 minutes of cooking, brush the roast with honey glaze every five minutes.

6. Serve

Remove the pork from the rotisserie spit and remove the twine trussing the roast. Be careful - the spit and forks are blazing hot. Let the pork rest for 15 minutes, then slice and serve.

Rack of Pork with Rosemary and Garlic Rub

"The closer to bone, the sweeter the meat" is an old cooking proverb. Bones give up their flavor to the surrounding meat as they cook, so I cook meat on the bone whenever possible.

Pork loin needs that extra flavor. Modern pork loin is very lean, almost pure protein. Fat carries flavor, and the fat has been bred out, so pork loin needs all the extra help it can get.

If you can find heirloom pork from a breed that still has a lot of fat, buy it! You won't be disappointed.

Ingredients

- 1 (4 pound) bone-in pork loin roast

Brine

- 3 quarts water
- 1/2 cup table salt (or 1 cup kosher salt)
- 1/4 cup brown sugar

Spice rub

- 4 cloves garlic, minced or pressed through a garlic press
- 1 teaspoon minced rosemary
- 1 teaspoon fresh ground black pepper
- 1/2 teaspoon hot red pepper flakes

Directions

1. Brine the pork

Combine the brine ingredients in a large container and stir until the salt and sugar dissolve. Submerge the pork in the brine. Store in the refrigerator for four to eight hours.

2. Rub, truss and spit the pork

One hour before cooking, remove the pork from the brine and pat dry with paper towels. Mix the rub ingredients in a small bowl, then rub over the pork shoulder, working the rub into any natural seams in the meat. Truss the pork roast, skewer it on the rotisserie spit, and secure it with the spit forks. Let the pork rest at room temperature until it is time to grill.

3. Set up the grill for indirect high heat

Set the grill up for indirect high heat with the drip pan in the middle of the grill.

4. Rotisserie cook the pork

Put the spit on the grill, start the motor spinning, and make sure the drip pan is centered beneath the pork roast. Close the lid and cook the pork until it reaches 135°F in its thickest part, about 45 minutes.

5. Serve

Remove the pork from the rotisserie spit and remove the twine trussing the roast. Be careful - the spit and forks are blazing hot. Let the pork rest for 15 minutes, then slice and serve.

Notes

- There are two ways to carve rack of pork. The easy way is to cut between the bones - each diner gets a thick chop with a bone attached. If you want smaller servings, cut the rack of bones off the roast, cut the rack of ribs into single bone pieces, and cut the roast into 1/2 inch slices.

Pork Loin with Honey and Thyme Glaze

Boneless pork loin is a neutral flavored lean protein. In other words...boring.

Booooooring.

We're going to help it out a bit. First, a brine seasons it all the way through. Next, we rub it with a spice rub. Then the rotisserie gives it a crackling crust, and wood smoke adds flavor. Finally, it is brushed with honey, cider vinegar and thyme, adding a sweet glaze to the outside. Boring pork loin? Not if I have anything to say about it.

Pork loin gets dry if it is overcooked. To prevent this, I double up the loin. I buy a four pound roast, cut it in half, and tie the two smaller pieces together. The doubled up meat adds thickness, slowing down the cooking. The slower cooking gives the outside of the roasts more time to brown.

Ingredients

- 2 (2 pound) boneless pork loin roasts

Brine

- 3 quarts water
- 1/2 cup table salt (or 1 cup kosher salt)
- 1/4 cup brown sugar

Spice rub

- 1 teaspoon coriander seeds, coarsely ground
- 1 teaspoon fennel seeds, coarsely ground
- 1 teaspoon garlic powder
- 1/2 teaspoon fresh black pepper, coarsely ground

Glaze:

- 1/4 cup honey
- 2 tablespoons cider vinegar
- 2 teaspoons minced fresh thyme (or 1 teaspoon dried thyme)

- Fist sized chunk of smoking wood (or 1 cup wood chips)

Directions

1. Brine the pork

Combine the brine ingredients in a large container and stir until the salt and sugar dissolve. Score the fat on the pork loins in a 1 inch diamond pattern. Submerge the pork in the brine. Store in the refrigerator for four to eight hours.

2. Rub, truss and spit the pork

One hour before cooking, remove the pork from the brine and pat dry with paper towels. Mix the spice rub ingredients in a small bowl, then pat the rub onto the pork. Truss the roasts together with the fat caps facing out, then skewer on the rotisserie spit, running the spit between the roasts and securing them with the spit forks. Let the pork rest at room temperature until it is time to grill. Submerge the smoking wood in water and let it soak until the grill is ready.

3. Make the glaze

Whisk the glaze ingredients in a small bowl.

4. Set up the grill for indirect high heat

Set the grill up for indirect high heat with the drip pan in the middle of the grill.

5. Rotisserie cook the pork

Put the spit on the grill, start the motor spinning, and make sure the drip pan is centered beneath the pork roast. Add the smoking wood to the fire, close the lid, and cook the pork until it reaches 135°F in its thickest part, about 50 minutes. During the last 15 minutes of cooking, brush the roast with glaze every five minutes.

6. Serve

Remove the pork from the rotisserie spit and remove the twine trussing the roast. Be careful - the spit and forks are blazing hot. Let the pork rest for 15 minutes, then slice and serve.

Pork Loin Rolled with Dried Fruit

I like to stuff boneless pork loins. The solid muscle of meat is easy to cut, and the boring neutral flavor means it will go with almost any stuffing. Pork and dried fruit are a classic combination, and I like to play up the fruit flavor with an apple cider brine.

Boring pork loin is a good thing if it is used to showcase other ingredients.

The hardest part of the recipe is roll cutting the loin. The trick is to cut most of the way through the loin, one third of the way up, without cutting all the way through. Then, fold open the pork at the cut like you are opening a book. Make another cut through the thick part of the roast, starting in the middle and cutting almost all the way through to the edge. Fold the second cut open, and the pork will be a flat piece of meat ready to stuff. Put a thin layer of stuffing on the cut surfaces, roll it back up, truss it, and it is ready for the rotisserie.

Ingredients

- 2 (2 pound) boneless pork loin roasts

Apple cider brine

- 2 quarts apple cider
- 1 quart water
- 1/2 cup table salt

Dried fruit stuffing

- 2 cups mixed dried fruit, chopped (apples, apricots, cranberries and raisins)
- 1 teaspoon fresh ground black pepper
- 1/2 teaspoon dried ginger

Directions

1. Brine the pork

Combine the brine ingredients in a large container and stir until the salt and sugar dissolve. Roll cut the pork roasts to open them up like a book. Set a roast with the fat cap facing down. Make a cut the length of the roast, one third of the way from the bottom, which goes almost all the way to the other side of the roast but not through. Open the roast up like a book along that cut, then make another cut halfway up the opened part of the roast, almost all the way to the other side, and open up the roast again. Submerge the pork roasts in the brine. Store in the refrigerator for one to four hours.

2. Stuff, truss and spit the pork

One hour before cooking, remove the pork from the brine and pat dry with paper towels. Open up the pork with the cut side facing up, and sprinkle evenly with the chopped fruit, ginger, and pepper. Carefully roll the pork back into a cylinder, then truss each roast at the edges to hold the cylinder shape. Truss the roasts together with the fat caps facing out, then skewer on the rotisserie spit, running the spit between the roasts and securing them with the spit forks. Let the pork rest at room temperature until it is time to grill.

3. Set up the grill for indirect high heat

Set the grill up for indirect high heat with the drip pan in the middle of the grill.

4. Rotisserie cook the pork

Put the spit on the grill and start the motor spinning. Make sure the drip pan is centered beneath the pork roast. Close the lid and cook the pork until it reaches 135°F in its thickest part, about 50 minutes.

5. Serve

Remove the pork from the rotisserie spit and remove the twine trussing the roast. Be careful - the spit and forks are blazing hot. Let the pork rest for 15 minutes, then slice into 1/2 inch thick rounds and serve.

Notes

- You can chop the dried fruit by hand, but pulsing it in a food processor is much easier.

- If roll cutting the pork sounds too difficult, then cut the pork roast in half lengthwise, fill with the stuffing, and truss the two halves back together. You'll lose a little more of the stuffing while cooking, and it won't have the cute stuffing spiral, but it will still taste amazing.

How to roll cut a pork loin

First cut

Second cut

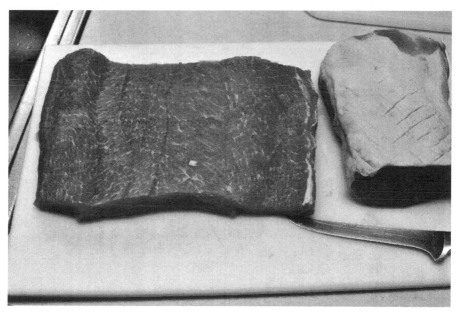

Third cut

Pork Loin with Pineapple, Mexican Style

Tacos al Pastor is the Mexican version of a gyro or shawarma, brought to Mexico City by Eastern Mediterranean immigrants. Thin sliced pork is marinated in an achiote based sauce, then stacked on a spit to form a thick loaf of meat, with a pineapple skewered on the end. The spit is attached to a vertical rotisserie, and pineapple juice drips down onto the pork as it spins. To serve, cooks slice thin pieces of pork and pineapple into corn tortillas.

I don't have a vertical rotisserie, and I skip the thin-slicing. I rub the whole loin with an achiote based spice rub, skewer the pineapple on the end, and cook it horizontally on my rotisserie.

Ingredients

- 2 (2 pound) boneless pork loin roasts
- 1 pineapple, trimmed and peeled

Brine

- 3 quarts water
- 1/2 cup table salt
- 1/4 cup brown sugar

Rub

- 1 tablespoon achiote powder (ground annatto)
- 1 teaspoon garlic powder
- 1 teaspoon ancho chile powder (or substitute a chili powder blend)

- 1/2 teaspoon ground cinnamon
- 1/8 teaspoon ground cloves

Accompaniments

- Tortillas
- Salsa
- Thin-sliced cabbage

Directions

1. Brine the pork

Combine the brine ingredients in a large container and stir until the salt and sugar dissolve. Score the fat on the pork loins in a 1 inch diamond pattern. Submerge the pork in the brine. Store in the refrigerator for four to eight hours.

2. Rub, truss and spit the pork and the pineapple

One hour before cooking, remove the pork from the brine and pat dry with paper towels. Mix the rub in a small bowl, then pat it onto the pork loins. Truss the loins together with the fat caps facing out, then run the spit between the roasts and secure the roasts with the spit forks. Poke a guide hole through the core of the pineapple with a thin, long-bladed knife. Skewer the pineapple on the spit. Let the pork and pineapple rest at room temperature until it is time to grill.

3. Set up the grill for indirect high heat

Set the grill up for indirect high heat with the drip pan in the middle of the grill.

4. Rotisserie cook the pork and pineapple

Put the spit on the grill, start the motor spinning, and make sure the drip pan is centered beneath the pork roast. Close the lid and cook until the pork reaches 135°F in its thickest part, about 50 minutes.

5. Serve

Remove the pineapple and pork from the rotisserie spit and remove the twine trussing the roast. Be careful - the spit and forks are blazing hot. Let the pork rest for 15 minutes. Slice the pork and pineapple and serve with tortillas, salsa, and thin-sliced cabbage.

Baby Back Ribs with Barbecue Dry Rub

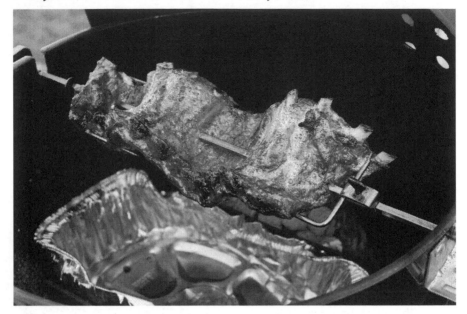

Ribs should cooked low and slow. The meat should melt off the bone. You don't need teeth to eat these ribs.

Um...no. I have a better way to cook ribs.

Spit roasted baby back ribs are a revelation. They have some bite to them, a contrast between the crisp outer crust and the tender meat between the bones.

Baby back ribs are attached to the pork loin - a tender cut of meat to begin with. They don't need the long, slow cooking that traditional barbecue uses to melt the connective tissue in tougher cuts, like spare ribs.

This is going to get the barbecue purists up in arms. I feel like I should apologize in advance...but I stand by my ribs.

Ingredients

- 1 slab baby back ribs

Brine

- 3 quarts water
- 6 tablespoons table salt (or 3/4 cup kosher salt)
- 1/4 cup brown sugar

Barbecue rub

- 1 teaspoon freshly ground black pepper
- 2 teaspoons paprika
- 2 teaspoons chili powder
- 1/2 teaspoon garlic powder
- 1/2 teaspoon onion powder
- 1/2 teaspoon dried thyme

Directions

1. Brine the ribs

Combine the brine ingredients in a large container and stir until the salt and sugar dissolve. Remove the membrane on the bone side of the ribs. To remove the membrane, slide a butter knife under the membrane, on top of one of the ribs. Use the knife as a lever to work the membrane off one of the bones. Once you have enough of the membrane loose, grab it with a paper towel and pull it off of the ribs. Submerge the slab of ribs in the brine, cover, and store in the refrigerator for one to four hours.

2. Spit the ribs

One hour before cooking, remove the ribs from the brine and pat dry with paper towels. Mix the rub ingredients in a small bowl, then sprinkle the and press the rub onto the ribs, concentrating on the meaty side. Weave the ribs onto the rotisserie spit, running the spit between every fourth bone on the rack. Secure the ends of the ribs with the rotisserie forks. Let the ribs rest at room temperature until it is time to grill.

3. Set up the grill for indirect medium heat

Set the grill up for indirect medium heat with the drip pan in the middle of the grill.

4. Rotisserie cook the ribs

Put the spit on the grill and start the motor spinning. Make sure the drip pan is centered beneath the ribs. Close the lid and cook until the ribs are well browned and the meat pulls back from the end of the bones by 1/2 an inch, about 1 1/2 hours.

5. Serve

Remove the ribs from the rotisserie spit. Be careful - the spit and forks are blazing hot. Brush the ribs one last time with barbecue sauce, then let the pork rest for 15 minutes. Slice into 2 bone pieces and serve.

Notes

- If you need sauce on your ribs, use the sauce from the Barbecued Chicken recipe. Brush it on a few times during the last fifteen minutes of cooking.

- When you are shopping for ribs, watch out for shiners - ribs that have the meat cut all the way down to the bone. If you can see bone, there won't be a lot of meat on the slab. Pick a slab without shiners if you can find it.

Baby Back Ribs, Chinese Restaurant Appetizer Style

Every Chinese-American restaurant has barbecued ribs on the appetizer menu. Go check the pu-pu platter at your local takeout place if you don't believe me. I'll wait...

Back so soon? See, I told you they'd be there. China loves pork, and spent centuries working out how to cook every part of the pig - including the ribs.

It's arrogant to think I can improve on centuries of tradition. But these ribs are inspired, crunchy and tender with a sticky, caramelized glaze. I'll bet your next order of Chinese ribs comes from your own backyard, not the hole-in-the-wall takeout place down the street.

Ingredients

* 1 slab baby back ribs

Marinade

* 1 cup soy sauce
* 2 tablespoons brown sugar
* 1 teaspoon five spice powder
* 1 teaspoon garlic powder
* 1/2 teaspoon cayenne pepper

- 1/2 cup peanut oil (or vegetable oil)

Glaze

- 3 tablespoons honey
- 3 tablespoons hoisin sauce
- 1 tablespoon seasoned rice vinegar
- 1 tablespoon soy sauce

Directions

1. Marinate the ribs

Remove the membrane on the bone side of the ribs. To remove the membrane, slide a butter knife under the membrane on top of one of the ribs. Use the knife as a lever to work the membrane off the bone. Once you have enough of the membrane loose, grab it with a paper towel and pull it off of the ribs. Mix the marinade ingredients in a gallon zip top bag. Fold the slab in half, put it in the bag, squeeze out all of the air, and seal the top. Flip the bag over a few time to coat the ribs with the marinade. Store in a baking dish in the refrigerator for one to four hours, flipping occasionally.

2. Spit the ribs

One hour before cooking, remove the ribs from the brine and pat dry with paper towels. Weave the ribs onto the rotisserie spit, running the spit between every third bone on the rack. Secure the ends of the ribs with the rotisserie forks. Let the ribs rest at room temperature until it is time to grill.

3. Make the glaze

Whisk the glaze ingredients in a medium bowl until smooth.

4. Set up the grill for indirect medium heat

Set the grill up for indirect medium heat with the drip pan in the middle of the grill.

5. Rotisserie cook the ribs

Put the spit on the grill and start the motor spinning. Make sure the drip pan is centered beneath the ribs. Close the lid and cook until the ribs are well browned and the meat pulls back from the end of the bones by 1/2 an inch, about 1 1/2 hours. During the last fifteen minutes of cooking, brush the ribs with glaze every five minutes.

6. Serve

Remove the ribs from the rotisserie spit. Be careful - the spit and forks are blazing hot. Brush the ribs one last time with glaze, then let the pork rest for 15 minutes. Slice into 2 bone pieces and serve.

Notes

- When you are shopping for ribs, watch out for shiners - ribs that have the meat cut all the way down to the bone. If you can see bone, there won't be a lot of meat on the slab. Pick a slab without shiners if you can find it.

- Make sure you have a dish under the marinating ribs. Sometimes a sharp bone will poke through the bag, and it is a real mess if you don't have something to catch the leaking marinade.

Ham with Maple and Brown Sugar Glaze

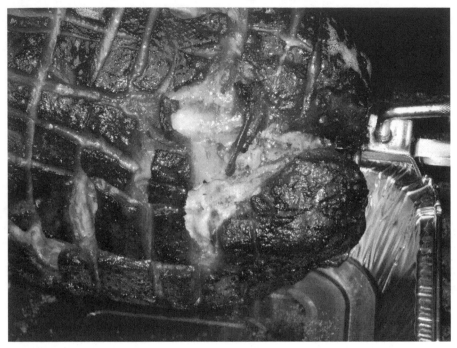

We're not cooking ham; it's already cooked. So, why bother with the rotisserie? Sure, you can reheat a ham in an oven-safe bag, if you're OK with steamed ham. I'll forgive you. Spiral sliced honey ham is easy.

But this ham is a show-stopper, with a crisped crust, melted pork fat, and sweet maple-brown sugar glaze. Yes, you'll have to do your own slicing. I'm sure your guests won't miss the perfect spiral slicing once they've had a taste. Make sure all the slices have a bit of the crust, and everyone will be thrilled.

Then there's the show off factor. When you bring the ham in from the grill, speared on the spit, crusty diamond pattern dripping with glaze...the guests will think you're a culinary genius. And all you did was reheat a ham.

Ingredients

- 1 (8 pound) bone in ham (shank or butt end)

Glaze

- 1/2 cup maple syrup (preferably Grade B maple syrup)
- 1/2 cup brown sugar
- 1/4 cup Dijon mustard

Directions

1. Score and spit the ham

One hour before cooking, remove the ham from its wrapper and pat dry with paper towels. Cut the rind of the ham in a 1 inch diamond pattern, cutting about 1/4 inch deep. Skewer the ham on the rotisserie spit, securing it with the spit forks. Let the ham rest at room temperature until it is time to grill.

2. Make the glaze

Whisk the glaze ingredients in a small bowl until the brown sugar dissolves.

3. Set up the grill for indirect medium-low heat

Set the grill up for indirect medium-low heat with the drip pan in the middle of the grill.

4. Rotisserie cook the ham

Put the spit on the grill, start the motor spinning, and make sure the drip pan is centered beneath the ham. Close the lid and cook the ham until it reaches 135°F in its thickest part, about 3 hours. During the last half hour of cooking, brush the roast with glaze every ten minutes.

5. Serve

Remove the ham from the rotisserie spit. Be careful - the spit and forks are blazing hot. Let the ham rest for 15 minutes, then slice and serve.

Notes

- Do not use a spiral sliced ham for this recipe. The juices will leak out of the pre-sliced ham, and it will dry out on the grill.

- Get a ham labeled "ham", "ham in natural juices", or "ham, water added". Avoid boneless "ham and water product", formed into a loaf shape, which is a pressed loaf that is so full of water it will never get a good crust.

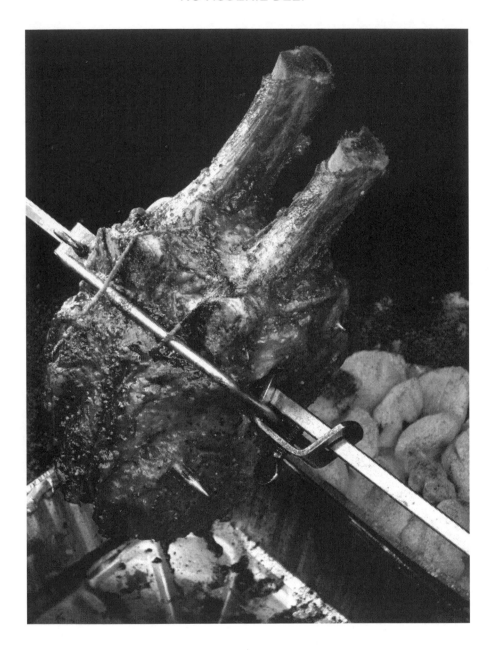

It is pitch black. The glow of the coals outlines a prime rib roast as it spins on the rotisserie. I fumble with my instant read thermometer and flashlight, wishing I had an extra set of hands, while snowflakes sizzle against the side of the grill.

It's Christmas. Why did I step out here in the cold and the dark, while everyone else celebrates inside? Because my family deserves a prime rib for Christmas, the best one I know how to make.

Beef cooking notes

I like my beef simple. Salt and pepper, wood smoke and the rotisserie. These recipes reflect that. Also, I like my beef medium-rare; the only exception is the rotisserie ribs, which need to be well done to be properly tender. Everything else I cook to 120°F, and let carry-over heat take the beef to rosy, pink and delicious medium-rare.

Prime Rib Roast

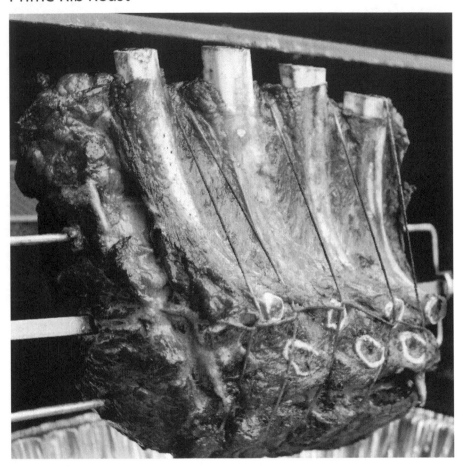

If you are feeding carnivores, this is the recipe to make. Rib roast is the best way to show off beef on the rotisserie. Cooked on the bone, seasoned with salt and pepper, served with horseradish sauce on the side. Simple and delicious.

I call this roast Prime Rib, and so do grocery stores, but most of the time that's not right. Prime rib has become a generic name for a beef rib roast, regardless of grade. When the USDA grades meat, only the top 2% is graded Prime. Almost all of the meat we buy in stores is graded Choice. The vast majority of Prime grade beef goes to high end steakhouses.

USDA Prime meat is amazing...if you are lucky enough to find it, and can afford it. I buy Choice roasts and save expensive Prime meat for the occasional steak.

I look for Certified Angus Beef, which grades out at the high end of Choice. Or I buy it from a local butcher who raises his own cattle. It never hurts to pay a little extra for good beef.

Grading is based on marbling - the amount of fat inside the muscle. Fat on the outside isn't as important; look for tiny veins of fat inside the meat. That interior fat melts during cooking, filling the beef with flavor. Prime meat is loaded with marbling. Choice meat is less marbled, but still has a decent amount of intramuscular fat.

Ingredients

- 1 (12 pound) bone-in beef rib roast (a four bone roast)
- 3 tablespoons kosher salt
- 1 1/2 tablespoons fresh ground black pepper

Horseradish sauce

- 1/2 cup sour cream
- 1/4 cup prepared horseradish
- 2 tablespoons Dijon mustard

- Fist sized chunk of smoking wood (or 1 cup wood chips)

Directions

1. Dry brine the beef

Season the rib roast with the salt and pepper. Refrigerate for at least two hours, preferably overnight.

2. Truss and spit the beef

One hour before cooking, remove the rib roast from the refrigerator. Truss the roast, then skewer it on the rotisserie spit, securing it with the spit forks. Let the beef rest at room temperature until the grill is pre-heated. Submerge the smoking wood in water and let it soak until the grill is ready.

3. Set up the grill for indirect medium-high heat

Set the grill up for indirect medium-high heat with the drip pan in the middle of the grill.

4. Rotisserie cook the beef

Put the spit on the grill, start the motor spinning, and make sure the drip pan is centered beneath the rib roast. Add the smoking wood to the fire, close the lid, and cook the beef until it reaches 120°F in its thickest part for medium-rare, about 2 hours. (Cook to 115°F for rare, 130°F for medium.)

5. Serve

Remove the rib roast from the rotisserie spit and remove the twine trussing the roast. Be careful - the spit and forks are blazing hot. Let the beef rest for 15 minutes, and while the beef is resting, whisk together the ingredients for the horseradish sauce. To carve the beef, cut the bones off of the roast, then slice the roast and serve.

Notes

- I pour the juices from my cutting board into a small serving dish to pass at the table.

- To make carving easier, have your butcher cut the ribs free of the roast. Truss the ribs back on to the roast before cooking. Removing the ribs ahead of time makes carving easier; just snip the trussing twine and you have a boneless roast ready to carve. (It also leaves the ribs as a chef's treat while carving the roast.)

- This is a large roast, to feed a crowd. Assume one pound of beef per person. Unless you have some dedicated carnivores...like my family. Then you should probably go with one bone per two people, and this roast will serve eight.

Rib Roast with Peppercorn and Garlic Crust

This is the French bistro classic, steak au poivre, scaled up to an entire roast.

I prefer this to real steak au poivre, actually. On a steak, the pepper coating overwhelms the beef. On a slice of rib roast, the balance is perfect, with the occasional bite of spicy crust lifting the flavor of the beef. If you like spicy food, however, get one of the slices from the end of the roast - it is loaded with pepper.

Ingredients

- 1 (5 pound) bone-in beef rib roast (a two bone roast)
- 1 1/2 tablespoons kosher salt

Rub

- 8 cloves garlic, minced or pressed through a garlic press
- 2 tablespoons mixed peppercorns, crushed

Directions

1. Dry brine the beef

Season the rib roast with the salt. Refrigerate for at least two hours, preferably overnight.

2. Rub, truss and spit the beef

One hour before cooking, remove the rib roast from the refrigerator. Rub the garlic and crushed pepper all over the rib roast. Truss the roast, then skewer it on the rotisserie spit, securing it with the spit forks. Let the beef rest at room temperature until the grill is ready.

3. Set up the grill for indirect high heat

Set the grill up for indirect high heat with the drip pan in the middle of the grill.

4. Rotisserie cook the beef

Put the spit on the grill, start the motor spinning, and make sure the drip pan is centered beneath the rib roast. Close the lid and cook the beef until it reaches 120°F in its thickest part for medium-rare, about 1 hour. (Cook to 115°F for rare, 130°F for medium.)

5. Serve

Remove the rib roast from the rotisserie spit and remove the twine trussing the roast. Be careful - the spit and forks are blazing hot. Let the roast rest for 15 minutes. Cut the bones off of the roast, slice the roast, and serve.

Notes

- Don't grind the peppercorns too fine. You want them cracked and in large chunks, not ground. I use my mortar and pestle to crush the peppercorns. If you don't have a mortar and pestle, you can improvise one, using a coffee mug as the mortar and a glass spice jar as the pestle. Or, use the largest setting on your pepper mill.

- If you can, have your butcher cut the bones from the roast, season the roast and bones separately, then truss them together for cooking.

Boneless Ribeye Roast

A ribeye has the big beefy flavor of a chuck roast, the tenderness of a tenderloin, the fatty juiciness of a short rib. It walks the fine line of perfection, combining the best parts of all the other cuts of beef, without any of their drawbacks.

Ignore the people who say they prefer tenderloin. Beef flavor? Hah! It's not there. Now, a porterhouse steak, then we have an argument.

Ribeye is a rib roast minus the ribs. It's simple - just slice and serve. If you're looking for an easy roast beef, this is the cut for you.

I'm cooking this ribeye the way I prefer my beef - salt, pepper, and the rotisserie. Nothing else. I want that perfect balance of beef to shine through.

Ingredients

- 1 (4 pound) boneless beef ribeye roast
- 1 tablespoon kosher salt
- 1 teaspoon fresh ground black pepper

Directions

1. Dry brine the beef

Season the rib roast with the salt and pepper. Refrigerate for at least two hours, preferably overnight.

2. Rub, truss and spit the beef

One hour before cooking, remove the rib roast from the refrigerator. Truss the roast, then skewer it on the rotisserie spit, securing it with the spit forks. Let the beef rest at room temperature until the grill is ready.

3. Set up the grill for indirect high heat

Set the grill up for indirect high heat with the drip pan in the middle of the grill.

4. Rotisserie cook the beef

Put the spit on the grill, start the motor spinning, and make sure the drip pan is centered beneath the rib roast. Close the lid and cook the beef until it reaches 120°F in its thickest part for medium-rare, about 1 hour. (Cook to 115°F for rare, 130°F for medium.)

5. Serve

Remove the rib roast from the rotisserie spit and remove the twine trussing the roast. Be careful - the spit and forks are blazing hot. Let the beef rest for 15 minutes, then carve and serve.

Ribeye Roast with Cajun Rub

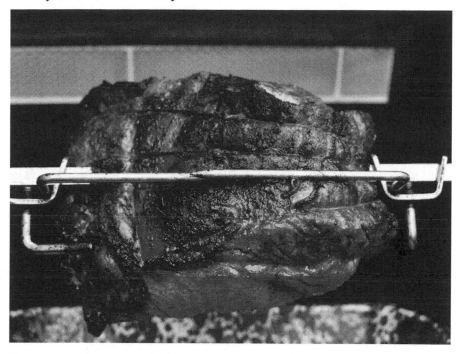

I've gone on long enough about simple beef roasts. Salt, pepper, beef flavor in all its glory, blah, blah, blah. Sometimes I need to kick things up a notch with a spicy Cajun rub.

*Bam!

**Sorry, too much Emeril as a young cook.

Sure, you can buy a Cajun spice blend at the grocery store. But why would you? Pick up a jar of that Cajun blend and look at the ingredient list. The first ingredient is always salt, which means there is more salt in the blend than anything else.

Why pay spice prices for salt? I make a big batch of Cajun rub and keep it in my spice rack. I'm prepared for any Cajun spicing emergencies in the kitchen.

*This is the same rub I use on my Cajun Turkey. Like I said, make a big batch - it will come in handy.

Ingredients

- 1 (4 pound) boneless beef ribeye roast
- 1 tablespoon kosher salt

Cajun rub

- 2 teaspoons paprika
- 2 teaspoons granulated garlic
- 1 teaspoon granulated onion
- 1 teaspoon fresh ground black pepper
- 1 teaspoon dried oregano
- 1 teaspoon dried thyme
- 1/2 teaspoon cayenne pepper
- Fist sized chunk of smoking wood (or 1 cup wood chips)

Directions

1. Dry brine the beef

Mix the Cajun rub ingredients in a small bowl, then season the rib roast with the salt and Cajun rub. Refrigerate for at least two hours, preferably overnight.

2. Truss and spit the beef

One hour before cooking, remove the rib roast from the refrigerator. Truss the roast, then skewer it on the rotisserie spit, securing it with the spit forks. Let the beef rest at room temperature until the grill is pre-heated. Submerge the smoking wood in water and let it soak until the grill is ready.

3. Set up the grill for indirect high heat

Set the grill up for indirect high heat with the drip pan in the middle of the grill.

4. Rotisserie cook the beef

Put the spit on the grill, start the motor spinning, and make sure the drip pan is centered beneath the rib roast. Add the smoking wood to the fire, close the lid, and cook until the roast reaches 120°F in its thickest part for medium-rare, about 1 hour. (Cook to 115°F for rare, 130°F for medium.)

5. Serve

Remove the rib roast from the rotisserie spit and remove the twine trussing the roast. Be careful - the spit and forks are blazing hot. Let the beef rest for 15 minutes, then carve and serve.

Notes

- If you take the easy way out, and use a store-bought Cajun spice blend, check where salt is in the ingredient list. If salt is the first ingredient (it probably is), skip the kosher salt and use the store-bought rub as the dry brine. If salt is the second or third ingredient, cut the kosher salt in half. After that, use the full tablespoon of salt in the dry brine. (And congratulations - you found a great spice blend!)

Beef Tenderloin with Herb Butter Baste

When you want to try a little tenderness, reach for the tenderloin.

*Tender is right there in the name, after all.

Unfortunately, tenderness comes with a price - lack of flavor. Tenderloin is very mild - the 98 pound weakling of beef roasts. It doesn't have much fat, and as I've mentioned before, fat carries flavor. I solve the problem by adding my own fat. Basting the tenderloin with herb butter adds a desperately needed layer of flavor.

The other problem is the tenderloin will cook through before it browns. I double up the roast, cutting it in half and tying the halves together. The doubled up roast takes longer to cook, giving the rotisserie extra time to develop a tasty brown crust.

Equipment

- Bundle of thyme and rosemary sprigs, tied into a basting brush

Ingredients

- 1 (5 pound) trimmed beef tenderloin (fat and chain removed, about 7 pounds untrimmed)
- 1 1/2 tablespoons kosher salt
- 2 teaspoons fresh ground black pepper

Butter baste

- 4 tablespoons (1/2 stick) butter
- 2 cloves garlic, minced or pressed through a garlic press
- 2 teaspoons minced fresh thyme
- 1 teaspoon minced fresh rosemary
- pinch of salt
- pinch of ground black pepper

Blue cheese and caper sauce

- 1/2 cup sour cream
- 1/4 cup crumbled blue cheese
- 1 tablespoon capers, drained and minced

Directions

1. Dry brine the beef

Season the rib roast with the salt and pepper. Refrigerate for at least two hours, preferably overnight.

2. Truss and spit the beef

One hour before cooking, remove the tenderloin from the refrigerator. Fold the tail of the tenderloin over and truss it to even out the thickness on the thin end of the roast. Cut the roast in half, truss the two pieces together, then skewer on the rotisserie spit, running the spit between the pieces of tenderloin and securing them with the spit forks. Let the beef rest at room temperature until it is time to grill.

3. Make the baste and the sauce

Heat the butter baste ingredients over medium heat in a small saucepan until the butter melts and the garlic starts to sizzle, about 5 minutes. (Or, microwave the butter and garlic for about 1 minute.) Whisk the caper sauce ingredients in a small bowl until the blue cheese and capers are thoroughly mixed with the sour cream.

4. Set up the grill for indirect high heat

Set the grill up for indirect high heat with the drip pan in the middle of the grill.

5. Rotisserie cook the beef

Put the spit on the grill, start the motor spinning, and make sure the drip pan is centered beneath the beef tenderloin. Close the lid and cook until the beef reaches 120°F in its thickest part for medium rare, about 40 minutes. (Cook to 115°F for rare, 130°F for medium.) During the last 15 minutes of cooking, brush the roast with the butter baste every five minutes, using the bundle of herbs as a brush.

6. Serve

Remove the tenderloin from the rotisserie spit and remove the twine trussing the roast. Be careful - the spit and forks are blazing hot. Let the tenderloin rest for 15 minutes, then slice and serve.

Beef Tenderloin with Porcini Rub and Red Wine Baste

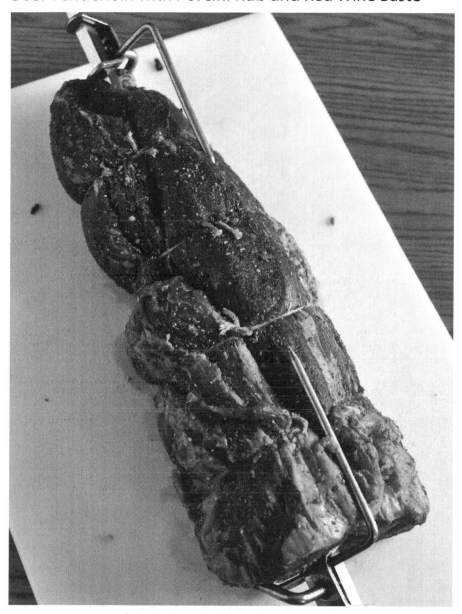

I believe in the hanging curveball, good scotch, and in seasoning beef with salt and pepper. Except for beef tenderloin. Tenderloin needs more than just salt and pepper.

How do I help a tenderloin? Umami. Umami is the fifth taste, the savor flavor discovered in Japan in the early nineteen hundreds. (It was added to the other four tastes we already knew - sweet, sour, bitter and salty.)

Meat has a lot of umami; so do seaweed, soy sauce, cabbage, tomatoes, and...mushrooms.

Mushroom powder is my secret weapon. I grind dried porcini mushrooms in the food processor and sprinkle them over the tenderloin with salt and pepper. The result is a unique spice crust and tenderloin with big beef flavor.

You don't have to tell anyone the flavor is a fungus among us.

Ingredients

- 1 (5 pound) trimmed beef tenderloin (fat and chain removed, about 7 pounds untrimmed)
- 1 1/2 tablespoons kosher salt
- 2 teaspoons fresh ground black pepper
- 1/2 ounce dried porcini mushrooms, ground to a powder

Red wine baste

- 2 tablespoons butter
- 2 tablespoons thin sliced shallot
- 1 cup red wine
- 1 sprig fresh tarragon
- pinch of salt
- pinch of ground black pepper

Directions

1. Dry brine the beef

Season the roast with the salt, pepper, and porcini powder. Refrigerate for at least two hours, preferably overnight.

2. Truss and spit the beef

One hour before cooking, remove the tenderloin from the refrigerator. Fold the tail of the tenderloin over and truss it to even out the thickness on the thin end of the roast. Cut the roast in half, truss the two pieces together, then skewer on the rotisserie spit, running the spit between the pieces of tenderloin and securing them with the spit forks. Let the beef rest at room temperature until it is time to grill.

3. Make the red wine baste

Heat the butter over medium heat in a small saucepan until it melts and stops foaming, then add the shallot and cook until softened, about 1 minute. Add the red wine, tarragon, salt and pepper, increase heat to medium-high and bring to a boil. Decrease the heat and simmer until the wine is reduced by half. Remove from the heat and discard the sprig of tarragon.

4. Set up the grill for indirect high heat

Set the grill up for indirect high heat with the drip pan in the middle of the grill.

5. Rotisserie cook the beef

Put the spit on the grill, start the motor spinning, and make sure the drip pan is centered beneath the tenderloin. Close the lid and cook the beef until it reaches 120°F in its thickest part for medium rare, about 40 minutes. (Cook to 115°F for rare, 130°F for medium.) During the last 15 minutes of cooking, brush the roast with the red wine baste every five minutes.

6. Serve

Remove the tenderloin from the rotisserie spit and remove the twine trussing the roast. Be careful - the spit and forks are blazing hot. Let the tenderloin rest for 15 minutes, then slice and serve, passing the remaining red wine baste as a sauce.

Sirloin Roast Wrapped with Bacon

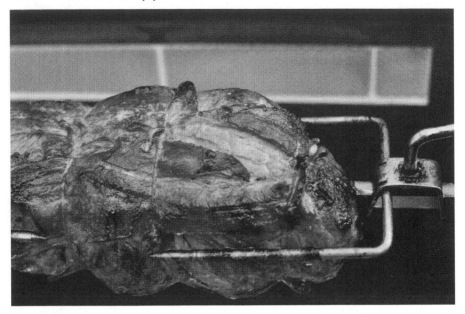

The rotisserie turns a less expensive roast into something great.

Get it? Turns? On the rotisserie? OK, I'll stop with the puns.

To help out an inexpensive roast, I wrap it in bacon. A little bacon never hurt, right?

The bacon must be tied down completely - no end pieces flapping around. Loose bacon is going to burn; if it is tight against the roast, it will be fine. If you do wind up with burnt edges, snip them off with kitchen shears. Or, remove the bacon after cooking, and serve the roast on its own.

Ingredients

- 1 (4 pound) sirloin roast
- 1 tablespoon kosher salt
- 4 slices bacon

Directions

1. Dry brine the beef

Season the roast with the salt, then refrigerate for at least two hours, preferably overnight.

2. Wrap with bacon, truss and spit the beef

One hour before cooking, remove the roast from the refrigerator. Cut the butcher's twine and lay the strings on a platter, spaced where you want to tie the roast. Put two slices of bacon on top of the string, with a gap between them. Put the sirloin on top of the bacon, then lay the last two pieces of bacon on top of the roast. Tie the twine to truss the roast and the bacon. Trim off any loose ends of bacon so they don't burn in the grill. Skewer the roast on the rotisserie spit, securing it with the spit forks. Let the beef rest at room temperature until the grill is ready.

3. Set up the grill for indirect high heat

Set the grill up for indirect high heat with the drip pan in the middle of the grill.

4. Rotisserie cook the beef

Put the spit on the grill, start the motor spinning, and make sure the drip pan is centered beneath the sirloin roast. Close the lid and cook the beef until it reaches 120°F in its thickest part for medium-rare, about 45 minutes. (Cook to 115°F for rare, 130°F for medium.)

5. Serve

Remove the sirloin roast from the rotisserie spit and remove the twine trussing the roast, leaving as much bacon behind as possible. Be careful - the spit and forks are blazing hot. Let the beef rest for 15 minutes, then carve into thin slices and serve.

Beef Ribs with Texas Dry Rub

Beef ribs are the bones that cover the prime rib. When you buy a boneless ribeye roast, these bones are the "waste". And it would be a waste to waste the bones.

If you're really lucky, your local butcher will treat them as waste and sell them cheap - I often find them for less than a buck a pound.

They aren't as popular as pork ribs, a former "waste" cut. Pork ribs are now more expensive than the meat they were attached to.

The ribs are sprinkled with a simple Texas style rub. Salt, pepper, and a little dried ancho chili to add some heat. There's nothing better than some big bones to gnaw on.

Ingredients

- 5 pounds (about 7 bones) beef back ribs

- Fist sized chunk of smoking wood (or 1 cup wood chips)

Spice rub

- 4 teaspoons kosher salt
- 2 teaspoons ground ancho chile pepper
- 1 teaspoon fresh ground black pepper
- 1/2 teaspoon ground chipotle chile pepper

Directions

1. Dry brine the ribs

Mix the spice rub ingredients in a small bowl. Remove the membrane on the bone side of the ribs. To do this, loosen the membrane by working a butter knife between the membrane and one of the bones on the end of the rack. Grab the membrane with a paper towel and pull it off of the ribs. Sprinkle and pat the rub on the ribs, concentrating on the meaty side. Refrigerate for at least two hours, preferably overnight.

2. Spit the ribs

One hour before cooking, remove the ribs from the refrigerator. Weave the ribs onto the rotisserie spit, running the spit between every third bone on the rack. Secure the ends of the ribs with the rotisserie forks. Let the ribs rest at room temperature until it is time to grill. Submerge the smoking wood in water and let it soak.

3. Set up the grill for indirect medium heat

Set the grill up for indirect medium heat with the drip pan in the middle of the grill.

4. Rotisserie cook the ribs

Put the spit on the grill and start the motor spinning. Make sure the drip pan is centered beneath the ribs. Add the smoking wood to the fire and close the lid. Cook until the ribs are well browned and the meat pulls back from the end of the bones by 1/2 an inch, about two hours.

5. Serve

Remove the ribs from the rotisserie spit. Be careful - the spit and forks are blazing hot. Slice between the bones and serve.

Notes

- Watch out for shiners - ribs that have the meat cut all the way down to the bone. If you can see the middle of the bones, there won't be a lot of meat on the slab. Pick a slab without shiners if you can find it.

Beef Tri-Tip

Santa Maria, California, has a unique style of barbecue. Tri-tip is rubbed with garlic salt, and grilled over red oak coals, giving it a hint of smoke flavor. The beef is sliced thin and served in sandwiches with salsa and red piquinto beans.

This is my take on grilled tri-tip. I shouldn't mention Santa Maria, actually. The Santa Maria Valley Chamber of Commerce has copyrighted the name "Santa Maria Barbecue" and they have a very specific recipe you have to follow. I'm sure I break all sorts of rules by using a rotisserie.

...But I'm willing to break a few rules for this beef...

Ingredients

- 2 pound tri-tip roast
- Fist sized chunk of oak smoking wood (or 1 cup wood chips)
- 2 teaspoons kosher salt
- 1/2 teaspoon fresh ground black pepper
- 1/2 teaspoon garlic powder

Garlic bread

- 1 loaf French bread, split lengthwise, then cut into sandwich size pieces

- 2 tablespoons butter
- 2 tablespoons olive oil
- 2 cloves garlic, minced or pressed through a garlic press

Directions

1. Dry brine the beef

Season the loin roast with the salt, pepper, and garlic powder. Refrigerate for at least two hours, preferably overnight.

2. Truss and spit the beef

One hour before cooking, remove the loin roast from the refrigerator. Skewer it on the rotisserie spit, securing it with the spit forks. Let the beef rest at room temperature until the grill is pre-heated. Submerge the smoking wood in water and let it soak until the grill is ready.

3. Set up the grill for indirect high heat

Set the grill up for indirect high heat with the drip pan in the middle of the grill.

4. Season the garlic bread

Heat the butter, olive oil, and garlic in a small saucepan over medium heat until the garlic starts to sizzle. Brush the garlic butter on the cut sides of the French bread.

5. Rotisserie cook the beef

Add the smoking wood to the grill, then put the spit on the grill and start the motor spinning. Make sure the drip pan is centered beneath the tri-tip. Close the lid and cook until the beef reaches 120°F in its thickest part for medium-rare, about 20 minutes. (Cook to 115°F for rare, 130°F for medium.)

6. Serve

Remove the loin roast from the rotisserie spit and remove the twine trussing the roast. Be careful - the spit and forks are blazing hot. Let the beef rest for 15 minutes. While the beef rests, put the garlic bread on the grill, cut side down, and toast until just browned, about one minute. (Watch the bread carefully - it goes from toasted to burned in a heartbeat.) Slice the beef thin and serve with the garlic bread.

Notes

- Tri-tip is a cut from the sirloin; if you can't find it, substitute a similar sized top sirloin roast.

Top Sirloin Steak Brazilian Churrasco Style (Picanha)

Picanha is the pinnacle of Brazilian churrascaria cooking. Top sirloin cap steaks with a thick layer of fat, spit-roasted over an open wood fire.

The tricky part is getting the right cut of meat from a non-Brazilian butcher. In America, no one has ever heard of Picanha. Ask for "a top sirloin cap roast with the fat cap still on it".

I took pictures downloaded from the Beef Checkoff website with me to the butcher. It was a good thing I did; I would have wound up with a tri-tip otherwise.

This cut is worth the extra effort. Beef-crazy Brazilians think picanha makes the best steaks...and I can't argue with them.

Ingredients

- 1 (3 pound) top sirloin cap roast with a thick layer of fat, cut across the grain into three steaks
- 4 teaspoons kosher salt

Directions

1. Season, truss and spit the beef

Bend each of the three steaks into a C shape, with the fat on the outside. Skewer the steaks with the spit and bracket with the spit forks to hold them in a tight C shape. Season with salt and let the steaks rest at room temperature until the grill is ready.

2. Set up the grill for indirect high heat

Set the grill up for indirect high heat with the drip pan in the middle of the grill.

3. Rotisserie cook the beef

Put the spit on the grill, start the motor spinning, and make sure the drip pan is centered beneath the steaks. Close the lid and cook the beef until it reaches 120°F in its thickest part for medium rare, about 20 minutes. (Cook to 115°F for rare, 130°F for medium.)

4. Serve

Remove the steaks from the rotisserie spit. Be careful - the spit and forks are blazing hot. Let the steaks rest for 15 minutes, then slice and serve.

Securing picanha on the spit

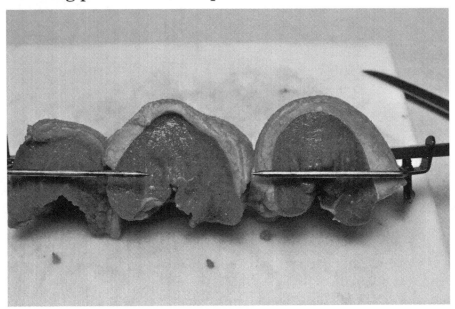

Americans eat less than one pound of lamb per person every year. I love lamb, and try to pull that average up all by myself. That doesn't mean the rest of you can slack off, however. In this chapter, I'll try to get you to join me.

If you make one of these recipes, you can do your part and double the national average in one night.

The strong flavor of lamb pairs well with other strong flavors - rosemary, thyme and mint; garlic and lemon; spice rubs with gusto. The rotisserie is both the perfect way to cook lamb and very traditional. Can't you picture lamb rotating on a spit right now?

I like my lamb cooked a little more than my beef. I aim for medium, 130°F, with a pink center. The exception, as always, is the hard-working lamb shoulder. It needs to be cooked to 190°F to turn this tough cut tender and juicy.

Whole Leg of Lamb with Greek Flavors

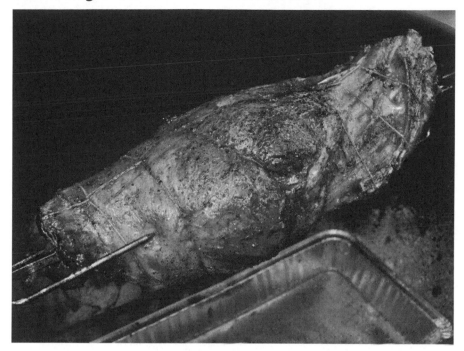

I watch movies for the cooking scenes. I know I'm biased, but I think the best scene in "My Big Fat Greek Wedding" is the party with a whole lamb roasting on a spit in the front yard.

Someday I'll cook an entire lamb, Greek style. Until then, I cook whole legs. I make a trip to the lamb specialists at the West Side Market in Cleveland, where can I get a whole leg with the shank bone cracked and folded back. That way I get to eat the shank as a chef's treat while I carve the lamb.

Ingredients

- 1 (8 pound) bone in leg of lamb

Greek rub

- 2 tablespoons kosher salt
- 3 cloves garlic, minced or pressed through a garlic press
- Zest of 1 lemon
- 1 teaspoon fresh ground black pepper
- 1 teaspoon dried oregano

Lemon garlic baste

- 1/4 cup olive oil
- Juice of 2 lemons
- 1 clove garlic, minced or pressed through a garlic press

Directions

1. Dry brine the lamb

Mix the rub ingredients in a small bowl, then season the leg of lamb with the rub, working it into any natural seams in the meat. Refrigerate for at least two hours, preferably overnight.

2. Truss and spit the lamb

One hour before cooking, remove the leg of lamb from the refrigerator. Truss the lamb, then skewer it on the rotisserie spit, securing it with the spit forks. Let the lamb rest at room temperature until the grill is ready.

3. Make the baste

Whisk the baste ingredients in a small bowl.

4. Set up the grill for indirect medium heat

Set the grill up for indirect medium heat with the drip pan in the middle of the grill.

5. Rotisserie cook the lamb

Put the spit on the grill, start the motor spinning, and make sure the drip pan is centered beneath the leg of lamb. Close the lid and cook the lamb until it reaches 130°F in its thickest part for medium, about 1 1/2 hours. (Cook to 115°F for rare, 120°F for medium-rare, or 140°F for medium-well.) During the last 15 minutes of cooking, brush the leg of lamb with the lemon baste every five minutes.

6. Serve

Remove the leg of lamb from the rotisserie spit and remove the twine trussing the roast. Be careful - the spit and forks are blazing hot. Let the lamb rest for 15 minutes, then carve and serve.

Notes

- The trick to this recipe is skewering the leg so it is balanced on the spit without running into the bone. Use the leg bone as a guide and run the spit right next to it.

Leg of Lamb with Moroccan Flavors

When I think of spit-roasted lamb, I picture a bazaar full of vendors shouting for your attention, with the smell of lamb wafting through the air.

Yes, I watch too many travelogues about Northern Africa. Like I said before, I'm watching for the food scenes.

This recipe is for a smaller lamb roast. I prefer the sirloin half of a lamb leg; it is the thicker end, with more meat on the bone. I rub the roast with a North African spice mix and baste it with lemon and honey. The sweet, spicy crust is incredible with the flavor of lamb.

Ingredients

- 1 (4 pound) bone in leg of lamb roast

Moroccan rub

- 1 tablespoon kosher salt
- 1 tablespoon paprika
- 2 teaspoons garlic powder (or 2 cloves minced garlic)
- 1 teaspoon fresh ground black pepper
- 1 teaspoon ground coriander
- 1 teaspoon ground cumin
- 1/2 teaspoon ground cinnamon

Honey baste

- 1/4 cup olive oil
- 1/4 cup honey
- Juice of 1 lemon
- 1 clove garlic, minced or pressed through a garlic press

Directions

1. Dry brine the lamb

Mix the rub ingredients in a small bowl, then season the leg of lamb with the rub, working it into any natural seams in the meat. Refrigerate for at least two hours, preferably overnight.

2. Truss and spit the lamb

One hour before cooking, remove the leg of lamb from the refrigerator. Truss the lamb, then skewer it on the rotisserie spit, securing it with the spit forks. Let the lamb rest at room temperature until the grill is ready.

3. Make the baste

Whisk the baste ingredients in a small bowl until the honey dissolves.

4. Set up the grill for indirect high heat

Set the grill up for indirect high heat with the drip pan in the middle of the grill.

5. Rotisserie cook the lamb

Put the spit on the grill, start the motor spinning, and make sure the drip pan is centered beneath the leg of lamb. Close the lid and cook the lamb until it reaches 130°F in its thickest part for medium, about 1 hour. (Cook to 115°F for rare, 120°F for medium-rare, or 140°F for medium-well.) During the last 15 minutes of cooking, brush the leg of lamb with the honey baste every five minutes.

6. Serve

Remove the leg of lamb from the rotisserie spit and remove the twine trussing the roast. Be careful - the spit and forks are blazing hot. Let the lamb rest for 15 minutes, then carve and serve.

Notes

- The spices in this rub will burn. If you are cooking on a gas grill, check the roast after a half an hour. If the roast is browning well, turn the heat down to medium for the rest of the cooking time.

Boneless Leg of Lamb with Tapenade Stuffing

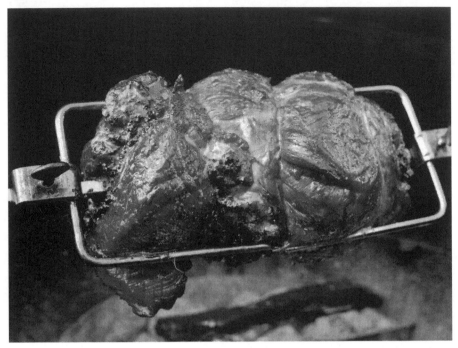

Boneless leg of lamb roasts come pre-butterflied, begging to be stuffed.

I'm stuffing the lamb with tapenade, the Provencal paste of olives, herbs and spices. I spent a week taking cooking classes in Provence, and this recipe immediately takes me back, puts me on a chair looking out over the Luberon, with a glass of Cotes du Rhone in my hand.

Open up the boned roast and spread the tapenade all over the inside of the lamb. Roll the roast back into its original shape, truss it, and we're ready for the rotisserie.

Ingredients

- 1 (2.5 pound) boneless leg of lamb
- 1 tablespoon kosher salt

Tapenade

- 1 clove garlic, peeled
- 2 basil leaves
- 1 cup (8 ounces) pitted Kalamata olives, rinsed
- 1 teaspoon capers
- Juice of 1/2 lemon

- 1/2 teaspoon fresh ground black pepper
- 1 anchovy fillet, rinsed (optional)
- 2 tablespoons grapeseed oil or vegetable oil

Directions

1. Dry brine the lamb

Season the leg of lamb with the salt, then refrigerate for at least two hours, preferably overnight.

2. Make the tapenade

Drop the garlic clove into a running food processor and process until completely minced. Turn the processor off, add the basil, and process with one second pulses until finely minced. Add the olives, capers, lemon juice, pepper, and anchovy. Process with one second pulses until finely minced, scraping down the sides of the bowl if necessary. Turn the processor on and slowly pour the oil through the feed tube into the running processor. Once all the oil is added the tapenade should be a thick paste. Use immediately, or store in the refrigerator for up to a week.

3. Stuff, truss and spit the lamb

One hour before cooking, remove the lamb from the refrigerator. Right before heating the grill, spread the tapenade over the cut side of the lamb, fold the roast back into its original shape, and truss it. (You're going to lose a little of the tapenade as you truss the roast; that's OK.) Skewer the lamb on the rotisserie spit, securing it with the spit forks. Let the lamb rest at room temperature until the grill is ready.

4. Set up the grill for indirect high heat

Set the grill up for indirect high heat with the drip pan in the middle of the grill.

5. Rotisserie cook the lamb

Put the spit on the grill, start the motor spinning, and make sure the drip pan is centered beneath the lamb. Close the lid and cook the lamb until it reaches 130°F in its thickest part for medium, about 45 minutes. (Cook to 115°F for rare, 120°F for medium-rare.)

6. Serve

Remove the lamb from the rotisserie spit and remove the twine trussing the roast. Be careful - the spit and forks are blazing hot. Let the lamb rest for 15 minutes, then carve and serve.

Notes

- Tapenade makes a great appetizer. Double the tapenade part of the recipe and reserve half of it before stuffing the lamb. Use the extra tapenade as a topping for rounds of french bread, pita bread, or crackers.

- Tapenade is easy to make, but if you want to save time, buy six ounces of tapenade from the store.

Boneless Leg of Lamb Stuffed with Feta and Herbs

Lamb is the centerpiece of Greek cuisine. Feta, olives, pine nuts, and lemon are the backbone of Greek flavors. In this recipe, I use those terms literally - the lamb will be the centerpiece, with a backbone of Greek flavors. Make this recipe and you'll swear you can see the island of Mykonos from your backyard.

Ingredients

- 1 (2.5 pound) boneless leg of lamb roast
- 2 teaspoons kosher salt

Feta stuffing

- 2 ounces crumbled feta cheese (about 1/2 cup)
- 1 teaspoon minced fresh rosemary
- 1 teaspoon minced fresh thyme
- Zest of 1/2 lemon

Directions

1. Dry brine the lamb

Season the leg of lamb with the salt, then refrigerate for at least two hours, preferably overnight.

2. Stuff, truss and spit the lamb

One hour before cooking, remove the lamb from the refrigerator. Just before heating the grill, mix the stuffing ingredients. Open up the lamb like a book, then spread the stuffing over the cut side of the lamb. Fold the roast back into its original shape. Truss the lamb, then skewer it on the rotisserie spit, securing it with the spit forks. (You're going to lose a little of the stuffing when you tie down the trussing twine; that's OK.) Let the lamb rest at room temperature until the grill is ready.

3. Set up the grill for indirect high heat

Set the grill up for indirect high heat with the drip pan in the middle of the grill.

4. Rotisserie cook the lamb

Put the spit on the grill, start the motor spinning, and make sure the drip pan is centered beneath the lamb. Close the lid and cook the lamb until it reaches 130°F in its thickest part for medium, about 45 minutes. (Cook to 115°F for rare, 120°F for medium-rare.)

5. Serve

Remove the lamb from the rotisserie spit and remove the twine trussing the roast. Be careful - the spit and forks are blazing hot. Let the lamb rest for 15 minutes, then carve and serve.

Notes

- If you are in a hurry, skip the fresh herbs and lemon zest. Use store bought pre-crumbled feta with garlic and herbs as the stuffing.

Lamb Shoulder with Mustard Herb Paste

I love shoulder cuts: tough, loaded with tough connective tissue. Cook them long enough and that connective tissue melts into lip smacking gelatin. Lamb shoulder is no exception; tough and chewy if undercooked, it turns juicy and tender with long cooking.

Lamb shoulder is harder to find than leg of lamb. I have to special order it from my grocery store, or make a trip to a local butcher who specializes in lamb. Check out your local ethnic markets and farmers markets - I'll bet you can find your own lamb specialist. Once you do, great lamb is a short shopping trip away.

Ingredients

- 1 (4 pound) boneless lamb shoulder roast

Mustard herb paste

- 1/4 cup whole grain mustard
- 1 tablespoon kosher salt
- 1 tablespoon minced fresh thyme
- 1 teaspoon minced fresh oregano
- 1 teaspoon minced fresh rosemary
- 1 teaspoon fresh ground black pepper

Directions

1. Dry brine the lamb

Mix the paste ingredients in a small bowl. Open up the lamb like a book, then rub all over with the paste, working it into any natural seams in the meat. Refrigerate for at least two hours, preferably overnight.

2. Truss and spit the lamb

One hour before cooking, remove the lamb from the refrigerator. Fold the lamb into its original shape, truss the lamb, and skewer it on the rotisserie spit, securing it with the spit forks. Let the lamb rest at room temperature until the grill is ready.

3. Set up the grill for indirect medium heat

Set the grill up for indirect medium heat with the drip pan in the middle of the grill.

4. Rotisserie cook the lamb

Put the spit on the grill, start the motor spinning, and make sure the drip pan is centered beneath the lamb shoulder. Close the lid and cook the lamb until it reaches 190°F in its thickest part, about 2 hours.

5. Serve

Remove the lamb shoulder from the rotisserie spit and remove the twine trussing the roast. Be careful - the spit and forks are blazing hot. Let the lamb rest for 15 minutes, then carve and serve.

Notes

- The herbs in this recipe are from a package of fresh poultry mix herbs at my local grocery store. You can substitute 2 tablespoons of whatever fresh herbs are available.

- Whole grain mustard is also called coarse grain, country style, or stone ground mustard. Look for a mustard that has a lot of whole seeds in it.

Lamb Shoulder with Mexican Spice Rub

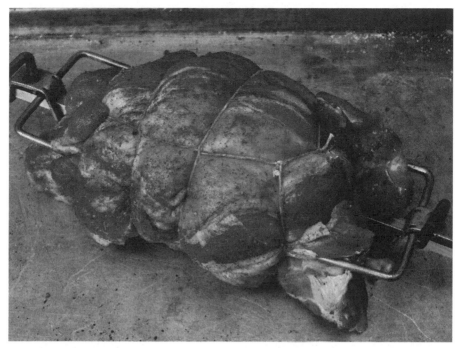

Barbacoa is a Mexican classic. The morning of a huge fiesta, lamb roasts are rubbed with chiles and spices, wrapped in banana leaves, and buried in a pit full of hot coals. After long, slow cooking in this huge earthenware oven, the lamb is dug up, unwrapped, sliced and served to the party guests.

Instead of a pit, I cook barbacoa over coals on my rotisserie. I know it would be more authentic in a pit. But, my wife is happier if I don't dig holes in the backyard and fill them with hot coals.

Ingredients

- 1 (4 pound) boneless lamb shoulder roast

Spice rub

- 1 tablespoon kosher salt
- 1 teaspoon fresh ground black pepper
- 1 teaspoon ancho chile powder
- 1/2 teaspoon garlic powder
- 1/4 teaspoon chipotle chile powder (or cayenne powder)
- 1/8 teaspoon (a pinch) ground cloves

- Fist sized chunk of smoking wood (or 1 cup wood chips)

Condiments

- Tortillas
- Salsa
- Shredded cabbage
- Minced cilantro
- Minced onions
- Lime wedges

Directions

1. Dry brine the lamb

Mix the spice rub ingredients in a small bowl. Open the boned lamb and rub all over with the spices, working them into any natural seams in the meat. Refrigerate for at least two hours, preferably overnight.

2. Truss and spit the lamb

One hour before cooking, remove the lamb from the refrigerator. Fold the lamb into its original shape, truss, and skewer on the rotisserie spit, securing the roast with the spit forks. Let the lamb rest at room temperature until the grill is pre-heated. Submerge the smoking wood in water and let it soak until the grill is ready.

3. Set up the grill for indirect medium heat

Set the grill up for indirect medium heat with the drip pan in the middle of the grill.

4. Rotisserie cook the lamb

Put the spit on the grill, start the motor spinning, and make sure the drip pan is centered beneath the lamb shoulder. Add the smoking wood to the fire, close the lid, and cook the lamb until it reaches 190°F in its thickest part, about 2 hours.

5. Serve

Remove the lamb shoulder from the rotisserie spit and remove the twine trussing the roast. Be careful - the spit and forks are blazing hot. Let the lamb rest for 15 minutes, then slice and shred into bite sized pieces. Serve the lamb with tortillas, salsa, shredded cabbage, and the other condiments on the side and let your guests make lamb tacos.

Rotisserie - it's not just for roasts any more.

You don't want all those delicious juices in the drip pan to go to waste, do you? Of course not. Make drip pan potatoes while the main course cooks on the rotisserie. And, if you have room on the spit, you can also skewer an onion and let it caramelize in the heat of the grill.

How about dessert? Yes, dessert on the rotisserie is a pineapple away. Sprinkle the pineapple with some sugar while it cooks, serve with ice cream, and your guests will think you're a grilling superhero.

Side dish cooking notes

If you are making a drip pan side dishes in a charcoal grill, watch out for ashes. Potatoes covered with pan drippings are awesome, but potatoes covered with ashes are awful.

Drip Pan Potatoes

Potatoes and rotisserie roasts are a natural combination. The potatoes sit under the roast and soak up all the delicious drippings. It's almost like making French fries, just healthier and better tasting.

But there is one problem: the drip pan is too far away from the heat, so the potatoes won't cook all the way through. I fix this by microwaving the potatoes to give them a head start. That way, the potatoes are mostly cooked, and they only have to brown in the drip pan.

Ingredients

- 2 pounds baking (russet) potatoes, peeled and sliced 1/2 inch thick
- 1 teaspoon kosher salt
- 2 teaspoons olive oil

Directions

1. Par-cook the potatoes

Toss the potatoes with the salt and olive oil in a microwave-safe bowl. Cover the bowl with plastic wrap and microwave the potatoes until they start to soften, about five minutes.

2. Start the roast

Set the grill up and start cooking the main dish on the rotisserie.

3. Cook the potatoes in the drip pan

When the main dish has about 45 minutes left to cook, carefully add the potatoes to the drip pan in an even layer. Cook the potatoes, stirring and flipping after 15 minutes, until the potatoes are well browned and crispy.

4. Serve

Remove the drip pan from the grill. Be careful - the pan will be hot. Remove the potatoes from the pan with a slotted spoon, letting the fat drip back into the pan. Taste the potatoes for seasoning and add salt and pepper if necessary.

Notes

- If you don't have a microwave, simmer the potatoes in a pot of salted water for ten minutes, or until just cooked through.

Drip Pan New Potatoes

I love roasted redskin potatoes, creamy on the inside and crunchy on the outside. This is the drip pan version, with the added bonus of rotisserie drippings.

The other reason I love redskin potatoes? I don't like peeling. The thin red skin on new potatoes is perfectly edible, making this a quick rotisserie side dish. Halve the potatoes, microwave them for five minutes to give them a head start on cooking, and then pour them in the drip pan. Stir occasionally. That's it.

I make this as a side dish almost every time I use the rotisserie. I feel like I'm being wasteful if I don't use the amazing juices that drip from a rotisserie roast.

Ingredients

- 1 1/2 pounds new potatoes, each potato cut in half
- 1 teaspoon kosher salt
- 2 teaspoons olive oil

Directions

1. Par-cook the potatoes

Toss the potatoes with the salt and olive oil in a microwave-safe bowl. Cover the bowl with plastic wrap and microwave the potatoes for five minutes, until they start to soften.

2. Start the roast

Set the grill up and start cooking the main dish on the rotisserie.

3. Cook the potatoes in the drip pan

When the main dish has about 45 minutes left to cook, carefully add the potatoes to the drip pan. Cook the potatoes, stirring and flipping every 15 minutes, until the potatoes are well browned and crispy.

4. Serve

Remove the drip pan from the grill. Be careful - the pan will be hot. Remove the potatoes from the pan with a slotted spoon, letting the fat drip back into the pan. Taste the potatoes for seasoning and add salt and pepper if necessary.

Notes

- If you don't have a microwave, simmer the potatoes in a pot of salted water until just cooked through, about ten minutes.

Drip Pan Sweet Potato Wedges

Drip pan sweet potatoes are a great match for pork or poultry, particularly turkey. It's a Thanksgiving thing - everyone has their favorite side dishes, and I demand sweet potatoes with my turkey.

*Turkey, gravy, mashed potatoes, stuffing, sweet potatoes. In that order. And the decoration on the table should be a cylinder of cranberry with the ridges from the can still visible. No, I'm not actually going to eat the cranberry cylinder, but it feels like it should be there. Kind of like a centerpiece for the table.

As with my other drip pan starches, I pre-cook the sweet potatoes in the microwave, slice them into wedges, and let them brown in the grill.

Sweet potatoes and yams are the same thing. What we call yams are a breed of sweet potato with orange flesh. Both work with this recipe - get whichever you prefer.

*Real yams are a large, white, starchy vegetable from Africa and Asia. They are closer to a potato than a sweet potato. For all I know they'll work in this recipe, but I've never seen one in person.

Ingredients

- 3 medium (10 ounce) sweet potatoes
- 1 teaspoon kosher salt

- 1/2 teaspoon fresh ground black pepper

Directions

1. Par-cook the potatoes

Microwave the sweet potatoes for eight minutes, or until they are cooked through and meet no resistance when pierced with a paring knife. Let them rest for a couple of minutes to cool down, then cut lengthwise into wedges. Season the cut sides with salt and pepper.

2. Start the roast

Set the grill up and start cooking the main dish on the rotisserie.

3. Cook the potatoes in the drip pan

When the main dish has about 45 minutes left to cook, carefully add the sweet potatoes to the drip pan, cut side up. Cook the sweet potatoes until they are well browned and crispy, moving them around in the drip pan if some of the sweet potatoes are browning too quickly.

4. Serve

Remove the drip pan from the grill. Be careful - the pan will be hot. Remove the sweet potato wedges from the pan with a slotted spoon or tongs, letting the fat drip back into the pan. Serve, giving each diner a couple of wedges of sweet potato.

Rotisserie Onion

If you have room on the end of the rotisserie spit, try a rotisserie onion. A medium onion will cook through in an hour. The onion will look hopelessly charred on the outside, but peel away the burnt exterior and you will find sweet, caramelized onions on the inside. They make a spectacular side dish for your rotisserie roast.

Now, pay more attention to the roast than the onions. It's OK if the onions overcook in fact, it's essential. Undercooked onions won't be sweet enough; overcooked onions just have an extra layer of char to remove before you get to the caramelized goodness hidden inside.

Ingredients

- 1 medium (8 ounce) onion, root and stem end trimmed but skin left on
- 1/2 teaspoon kosher salt

Directions

1. Spit the onion

Spit and secure the main course, then skewer the onion through the root end, pushing it right up against the spit fork holding the main course. If you have an extra spit fork, use it to secure the onion to the spit.

2. Set up the grill for indirect high heat

Set the grill up for indirect high heat with the drip pan in the middle of the grill.

3. Rotisserie cook the onion

Put the spit on the grill, start the motor spinning, and make sure the drip pan is centered beneath the main course. Close the lid and cook until the onion is blackened on the outside and tender all the way through, about 1 hour.

4. Serve

Remove the onion from the rotisserie spit. Be careful - the spit and forks are blazing hot. Cut the blackened skin away from the onion and discard. Dice the cooked onion, sprinkle with salt, and serve.

Rotisserie Pineapple

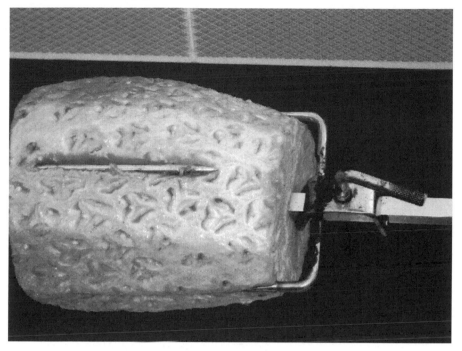

Rotisserie Pineapple may seem exotic, but caramelized pineapple sprinkled with cinnamon sugar makes a killer dessert.

Put the pineapple on your spare spit, put it on the grill when you take off the main course, and you'll have dessert finishing up right when you need it.

And...just kidding. Most people aren't as rotisserie crazy as I am, with an extra spit lying around.

I cook the pineapple on my one spit, at the same time as the main course. It goes on the end of the spit, right next to the roast, so dessert is done at the same time as dinner. Serve as a sweet side dish with dinner, or save the pineapple for dessert and serve it with a scoop of good vanilla ice cream.

Ingredients

- 1 pineapple, trimmed and peeled
- 1/4 cup sugar
- 1/4 teaspoon cinnamon

Directions

1. Spit the pineapple

Poke a guide hole through the core of the pineapple with a thin, long-bladed knife. Skewer the pineapple on the spit, securing it with a spit fork. Mix the sugar and cinnamon in a small bowl.

2. Set up the grill for indirect high heat

Set the grill up for indirect high heat with the drip pan in the middle of the grill.

3. Rotisserie cook the pineapple

Put the spit on the grill, start the motor spinning, and make sure the drip pan is centered beneath the pineapple. Close the lid and cook until the pineapple is softened and starting to brown, about 45 minutes. During the last 15 minutes of cooking, sprinkle the pineapple with cinnamon sugar every five minutes.

4. Serve

Remove the pineapple from the rotisserie spit. Be careful - the spit and forks are blazing hot. Let the pineapple rest for 10 minutes, then slice and serve.

Notes

- If you want to be thorough, use a cookie cutter to core out each pineapple ring before serving.

BIBLIOGRAPHY AND SUGGESTED READING

Rotisserie Recipes

As I said in the opening, cookbooks with rotisserie recipes are few and far between. Here are the cookbooks and articles that fed my rotisserie obsession:

Parsons, Russ. "It's Roasting Outside." *Los Angeles Times*. 16 July 2003.

Purviance, Jamie. *Weber's Big Book of Grilling*. Oxmoor, 2001.

Purviance, Jamie. *Weber's Real Grilling*. Oxmoor, 2005.

Purviance, Jamie. *Weber's Way to Grill*. Oxmoor, 2009.

Raichlen, Steven. *How To Grill*. Workman, 2001.

Raichlen, Steven. *BBQ USA*. Workman, 2003.

Raichlen, Steven. *The Barbecue! Bible*. Workman, 2008.

Raichlen, Steven. *Planet Barbecue!* Workman, 2010.

Steingarten, Jeffrey. "As the Spit Turns." *It Must've Been Something I Ate*. Knopf, 2002.

General Cooking information

As I said in my introduction - everything I do is built on the shoulders of those who came before me. Here are the food books that influenced this one the most.

Anderson, Pam. *How to Cook Without a Book*. Clarkson Potter, 2000.

Bayless, Rick. *Rick Bayless's Mexican Kitchen*. Scribner, 1996

Brown, Alton. *Good Eats*. Food Network, 1999-2012.

Kimball, Christopher, et al. *Cooks Illustrated Magazine*. Boston Common Press, 1993-today.

Lopez-Alt, J. Kenji. "The Food Lab." SeriousEats.com, 2009-today.

<http://www.seriouseats.com/the-food-lab>

McGee, Harold. *On Food and Cooking*. Scribner, 2004.

Page, Karen and Dornenburg, Andrew. *The Flavor Bible*. Little, Brown, 2008

Rodgers, Judy. *The Zuni Cafe Cookbook*. W. W. Norton, 2002.

Ruhlman, Michael. *Ratio*. Scribner, 2009

ABOUT THE AUTHOR

Hi! I'm Mike Vrobel, and I'm obsessed about home cooking. I spend all my free time thinking about cooking, reading about cooking, or writing about cooking. Oh, and actually cooking, too - I make dinner for my family every night.

I live with my wife, Diane, and our three children, Ben, Natalaie, and Tim, in Copley, Ohio.

Questions? Comments? Interested in more recipes and videos? Visit me at my website, <u>DadCooksDinner.com</u>.